CONCILIUM

concilium 1993/2

ANY ROOM FOR CHRIST IN ASIA?

Edited by

Leonardo Boff and Virgil Elizondo

SCM Press · London
Orbis Books · Maryknoll

Published by SCM Press Ltd, 26–30 Tottenham Road, London N1
and by Orbis Books, Maryknoll, NY 10545

April 1993

ISBN: 0 334 03019 6 (UK)
ISBN: 0 88344 870 X (USA)

Typeset at The Spartan Press Ltd, Lymington, Hants
Printed by Mackays of Chatham, Kent

Concilium Published February, April, June, August, October, December

Contents

Editorial

Christ in Asia: Some Aspects of the Struggles

Our Vietnamese author, Mai Thành, personalizes the very heart of the struggle of this issue when she tells us the story of her conversion. When she informed her father that she wanted to become a Christian, his response was: 'If you become a Catholic, we can no longer live under the same roof. One of us will have to leave this home.' This has been the struggle of millions of converts in all parts of the world beyond the West. Does Christianity come to divide and break up families, to destroy ancient traditions of life, to eradicate the wisdom of the ancients and desecrate sacred rituals of peoples? If this is the case, it would appear more as a perverse religion of destruction and division than one of life and unity. This certainly does not seem like the religion of Jesus who prayed that all might be one, but never prayed that all might be the same! The old Christian world of the West is today being challenged by the spiritual children of the hundreds of years of missionary activity from the West to discover new aspects of Christianity which have remained hidden and unsuspected.

Working on this issue of *Concilium* has been a great experience, which has taken me back to 1968, when I spent a year at the East Asian Pastoral Institute in Manila studying Christianity from within the midst of various Asian experiences. It was the first time I had ever left Western civilization. I had never realized how many Western notions I had simply taken for granted, assuming that they were of the essence of my Christian faith and perfectly understandable to anyone around the world. I was operating out of the naive notion that if we just translated correctly, everyone would understand! I did not even begin to suspect that there were totally different worlds of understanding reality that did not even have the most basic concepts or words which were fundamental in either Spanish or English.

Living, studying, discussing, searching and partying with persons from Pakistan, Taiwan, Thailand, Japan, India, Sri Lanka, Indonesia, Vietnam and many other places opened my eyes and my heart to many marvellous ways of understanding reality and my Christian religion that I had never suspected. Many of my unsuspected presuppositions were questioned and challenged, but far from threatening me or my Christian faith, the confrontations with the other cultures and religions gave me new insights into my own self as a Westerner and as a Christian. I was dying to my absoluteness as a Western Christian but was arising more human and more Christian.

It quickly became evident how impoverished Western Christianity had become by encasing itself in its own Western mind-sets and not allowing itself to be enriched by the wealth of knowledge and understanding of other peoples of the world. Worse than that, we had often kept the refreshing newness of the gospel from coming through because we had insisted so much on our linguistic/philosophical/theological presentations based on our Western cosmovision rather than trusting the dynamism of the gospel stories and imagery which would have easily entered into dialogue with the life-stories of any cosmovision in the world.

1942 marked the birth of colonial Christianity on a world-wide scale. The great Western expansion was characterized by the unquestioned syncretistic mixture of the gods of Mammon and the Christian God of eternal life. Since the Constantinian inversion, this syncretism had been developing in Western Christianity. The Empire and the Kingdom were fused into one coherent though deeply contradictory cosmovision. In this strange synthesis, there was a curious mixture and interdependency of God and gold, material wealth and salvation, earthly property and heaven, charity and cruelty, love and violence, enslavement and emancipation, military power and spiritual power, church and state. This European religious syncretism produced a mixture of imagery which interwove (rather than opposed, as the Gospels did) the Roman Empire and all its power, might, pomp and grandeur with the Kingdom of God and its renunciation of power and call to poverty, self-sacrifice for the sake of others, and childlike simplicity. Those who belonged to the Empire-Kingdom considered themselves saved and civilized. All others were considered heathen and uncivilized. The Empire called for conquest and domination while the Kingdom called for renunciation and service. Yet these two contradictory notions of life became the basis of the syncretistic Christianity of the West which would allow it to destroy and defend, wound and seek to heal, exterminate and seek to offer life, but in the end enslave, exploit, abuse and kill – all for the greater honour and glory of God. Can colonizing Christianity renew itself from within? I do not think that this is possible. The tradition of arrogance is too deeply ingrained for

instance, and new possibilities provided for more fruitful dialogue with our Jewish sisters and brothers in the future.

Not all accounts of a complex historical development can be expected to agree, especially when differing methodological approaches are adopted by scholars who address the issue with different concerns. Thus in the biblical section there is an inevitable overlapping as differing opinions surface about the origin and continued expression of belief in the Messiah within the biblical witness, depending on whether the author's focus is on the Hebrew scriptures (Beuken), extra-canonical Jewish writings (Horsley), or the New Testament (Freyne). These differences, especially between Beuken and Horsley, are based, partially at least, on the different perspectives of the authors – the former adopting a literary and the latter a sociological approach – the former concentrating on the world of text, the other on the world behind the text. For Beuken belief in the Messiah originated in the pre-exilic period, as can be seen in the treatment of the figure of 'Yahweh's anointed' in the Books of Samuel and the Psalms. This figure serves as an ideal against which the failings of the house of David are to be measured and becomes a cipher to express Israel's longing for complete redemption which it did not experience in and through the monarchy, thus enabling it to overcome the trauma of the exile. It is, therefore, a product of Israelite prophetic consciousness dating from the pre-exilic period, not an import of Near Eastern royal ideology as Horsley claims, by which the Davidic monarchy itself sought to legitimate its own position over against notions of what he calls 'popular kingship'.

Horsley's sociological approach, based on a theory of conflict, by which competing groups are seen to generate their own ideology of legitimation and liberation, finds ample evidence in the later biblical writings and other extra-canonical Jewish literature of the Second Temple period. In this regard the writings of the Jewish historian, Flavius Josephus, are particularly important in that from these one can glean echoes at least of alternative, popular movements to those represented by the scribal class who produced the bulk of the literature for upper classes. The survey of this diverse body of literature will surprise many who have been brought up to believe that expectation of the Messiah was the hallmark of Jewish faith in the period. In Horsley's account (as distinct from Beuken) the scattered references to the Messiah, even in Qumran, form no systematic or well-established pattern in terms of an expected Davidic end-time liberator. For him, the movements of popular kingship form the best analogue to the Jesus movement, whereas apocalyptic and other images of a transcendent figure are significant for later Christian reflections about the special significance of Jesus.

Important as this challenging corrective is to the standard Christian account of Jewish expectations, it runs the risk of erring in the opposite direction. Certainly, the New Testament writings, especially the Gospels, point to a variety of expectations and speculations about the Messiah in contemporary Jewish circles. This is the point of departure of the article by Freyne, who seeks to allow these New Testament writings to speak to the issue in their own terms. There are undoubtedly different emphases in the formulation of Jesus' messianic role, which is nevertheless, affirmed in all the writings. These differences can be explained in relation to the larger concerns of the writers, often in polemical contexts with competing Jewish groups, but also with reference to the social concerns of the various Christian groups being addressed. While agreeing with Horsley that we must avoid synthetic constructions of the Messiah that have more to do with Christian theology than actual, first-century, historical realities, Freyne would, nevertheless, see that the issue of the Messiah was more 'in the air' than one might suspect from a reading of Horsley's article. At the same time the variety of early Christian usage of the idea and the concern to integrate it with other images and symbols of liberation point to the probing, exploratory nature of early Christian confessions about Jesus' messianic status, rather than the absolute and definitive claims that have been made by Christian orthodoxy.

The issue of diversity of emphasis in different documents continues to be the concern of Jacob Neusner's pioneering work in the field of rabbinic scholarship. The absence of the Messiah in the foundation document of that corpus, the Mishnah, can be explained, partly at least, in terms of the political failures of the two 'messianic' wars against Rome (66–70 and 132–135 CE). The sages who framed the Mishnah were concerned to develop an alternative system for Israel, based on sanctification through order rather than salvation through militant, human action. The challenge to Israel is to fashion a life-style that would seek to ignore the vicissitudes of history. Yet memories of history, especially sorrowful ones, do not readily depart, so by the fourth century, Israel turned back to its history in order to learn the lessons of history in the Talmud of the land of Israel (Yerushalmi). Israel can never be autonomous; there is only a choice of master: God or the nations. Once that lesson of history has been learned, then the Messiah myth can return as part of Israel's history, as it does in this great collective work. However, the role of the Messiah is now utterly changed, in line with the fundamental philosophy framed by the Mishnah world, many of the original image-metaphors of the Gospels lost out to the highly rationalized philosophical notions which tried to explain the truth of Christianity according to a new cosmovision. This was helpful to some, but would become detrimental to others. Today, the new insights that are coming from the brokenness of Asia, Africa, Latin America and the oppressed minorities of the world will allow Christians universally to continue their pilgrimage unto the fullness of truth – a truth that is so rich that it cannot be contained adequately in any one cosmovision but which will be better comprehended as it is seen through the various mind-sets of today's world. We trust that this issue of *Concilium* will help open new possibilities of understanding – of ourselves and of others.

It is fitting that we should close the issue with the article of Tissa Balasuriya, who has been one of the pioneering Asian voices for many years. Tissa has long brought new hope for his own people as he has challenged us in the West to let go of our securities, go beyond our religious labels and discern the fruits of God's spirit which is at work in religions and secular ideologies which are seeking the true betterment and liberation of the oppressed of the world. It is tragic that our religious institutions, rather than helping this process along, are often, in their typical insecurity, impeding it. But the Spirit is greater. The celebration of the Workers' Mass of the Christian Workers Fellowship is a moving expression of the truly universal and all inclusive religious feast of the exciting new things which are emerging out of the sufferings of Asia.

We express our deep gratitude to our Asian colleagues, A. Pieris and Mary John Mananzan, and to the members of the Ecumenical Association of Third World Theologians for their close collaboration in putting this issue together.

Virgil Elizondo, with
Leonardo Boff

I · Background

Some Guises of 'Christ' in Asia

Teotonio R. de Souza

Jesus became a saving experience for some Semitic Jewish Asians to start with, and to several others. He was proclaimed as the Christ in the New Testament and by the post-apostolic churches ever since. However, the New Testament has no single orthodox christological model. Its christology was 'inclusive and pluriform', to quote an expression of the scripture scholar George-Soares Prabhu at the recent General Assembly of EATWOT in Nairobi (January 1992). The post-apostolic churches not only lacked a consensus about their christologies, they even displayed a violent disagreement about them, as witnessed by the turbulent controversies of the Constantinian and post-Constantinian times. Hence it may be unfair to reduce God's salvific manifestations in the history of all Semitic people and many other children in Asia and the rest of the world to the images and at times caricatures of Christ manufactured and exported by the dogmatic theologies understandable or acceptable to the Western mind and to the socio-political systems backing them.

The minority complex of the Jews and similarly the minority complex of Western civilization, particularly since the period of 'discoveries' and the beginning of 'world capitalism', are greatly responsible for an unhealthy globalization of Christ, which seeks wittingly or unwittingly to deprive him from his 'incarnation' and to reduce him instead to a 'universal uniqueness'. It had to be an incarnation of the values and ways of life acceptable to the 'missionary' church or churches of the West, instead of responding to the native understanding of Jesus and its cry for life. In an open-ended christology Jesus could freely assume a title or titles different from any borrowed from the titles known to the West or needing its approval. There have been some historical exceptions to this, however timid and boldly suppressed. But since Vatican II it was hoped that the exceptions would become a rule that would help recognize the genuineness of the Christ-experiences of the Asian peoples and accept their various names for them, rather than suspecting them and subjecting them to the test of the theological fine art and hair-splitting doctrines of the West.

The traditional capitalist mentality of the Jews, which has become co-natural to the development of the Western mind and its socio-political-economic structures, has sought to present Christ to the rest of the world, including Asia, as yet another monopoly good of its global market. As a result their Christ remains to a great extent an intruder, not an Asian Christ. The churches preaching such a Christ have remained largely churches *in* Asia, and have failed to be churches *of* Asia. Instead of joining the great religions of Asia as co-workers in the mission to the millions of *poor*, the missionary churches in Asia look upon them as rivals and threaten its 'uniqueness' and the 'uniqueness' of their Christ-product. As long as these churches fail to die with Christ to their search for wealth and power, they are not likely to rise with him and communicate the life of his risen Spirit to the millions of Asian poor experiencing the forces of death in their daily lives. The 'foreign funds' and the political power behind the Western church structures have not succeeded after centuries in winning over more than an insignificant percentage of the God-loving and deeply spiritual Asian masses. The concept and, worse still, the reality of the universal and Catholic church is often in practice reduced to universality of jurisdictional power and visible in the way this power is used to chastize any questionings of its authority or its policies that are often visibly and invisibly in service of the world capitalist structures and interests. There was a time when the Cold War and the concomitant balance of forces permitted a semblance of a church that was beginning to live up once again to its prophetic origins and mission. However, the more recent developments and the New Order promised by them are also showing their impact on the church. The Christ-product of this situation could once again revive and exacerbate the old conflicts and rivalries, thereby making the reality of Christ's incarnation in Asia a continued mystery for the Asians to live and draw their strength from.

The Syrian Christ of St Thomas Christians

Whatever the emphasis that is placed on the importance of oral traditions in the Eastern cultures and the reliability of the methods of preserving such traditions with a sacredness attached to them *vis-à-vis* the Western cultures that lived in a climate that enabled them to depend on writing materials, doubts can be still legitimately raised about the historicity of the arrival of St Thomas in India in person. At least the tradition of St Thomas converting Brahmin families appears anachronistic, because the Aryanization of Kerala and the caste-stratification had to wait for some more centuries. Despite the existing indications of Roman trade with peninsular India and the presence of Jewish settlements there to explain the arrival of the Apostle, there has been a long tradition of influences upon that sub-continent through the north-western land borders. The campaign of Alexander the Great to the Indus region and the Hellenistic influences in Indian art and culture are one such example. It is very probable that it was the conflict between the Roman and the Persian empires in the early centuries of the Christian era, and the consequent problem of loyalties for the churches of the Middle East, in the early fifth century, that led some of these churches, including those depending on Antioch, to assert their autonomy on the basis of apostolic traditions. The East Syrian or Chaldean church thus developed as an autonomous centre of church expansion and it had to pay the price of being dubbed 'Nestorian' by the rival churches of the West. Incidentally, the early christological 'heresies' and the 'Eastern schism' also need to be understood in the context of the conflict resulting from the cultural-political inferiority complex of the Rome-based papacy and the church authorities functioning in the aura of the imperial glow of Byzantium. Rome sought to make up for its complex by over-asserting itself juridically. One should also beware of the constant use of the term 'East' in the early church histories written in the West. It is not so much the *East*, but east of the West! It was the Mediterranean east of the Greek Byzantine cultural world. Perhaps the real East began to manifest its identity through the Chaldean Syrian language, thereby making its 'Monophysist' categories less understandable to the Latin and Greek West. The Syrian church broke away into the West Syrian Monophysite or Jacobite church in reaction to the Council of Chalcedon, and into the East Syrian or the Nestorian church after the council of Ephesus.

The school of Nisibis-Edessa was perhaps the greatest centre of learning and of spiritual dynamism of early Christianity. It moulded early Christianity in the East. Edessa (modern Urfa in Turkey) was on the trade route between Syria and Armenia. Merchants from China and India passed through Edessa to the West. Nisibis (now Nusaybin in Syria, and located north-east of Mosul) was also an important commercial centre and militarily strategic. As such it often changed hands between the Persians and the Romans. The theological school of Nisibis-Edessa (so-called for being shifted between these two places with changes of political masters) was established soon after the council of Nicaea, and neither Alexandria nor Antioch, much less Rome, came anywhere close to its level of fame.

While the Monophysite church withstood both the intolerance of Byzantine Christianity and of Islam, the East Syrian Church showed great missionary activity, not only within the kingdom of Persia among the Iranian population of Mazdean religion, but even beyond in India and Central Asia as far as China. From the fourth century, possibly the Persian persecutions and later the Islamic pressures pushed many groups of the Syrian Christians ascribing apostolic origin (St Thomas) to their church further east. The tradition of Thomas of Cana and others coming from Syria is well preserved among the St Thomas Christians of south India. However, their linkage with China via India has also been suggested. The discovery of a stone inscription at Hsianfu, which was capital of north China, points to the existence of Christianity in China in the seventh/ eighth centuries. The inscription in Chinese and Syriac, plus the existence of Jewish colonies and trade contacts between China and India, including Mylapore on the Coromandel coast, seem to add credibility to the Syrian Christian linkage of India and China. There were also Buddhist monks going to China from India in the second and third centuries, and we know of Hiuen-Tsang, Chinese scholar and Buddhist monk, who came to the court of Harsha in the seventh century and spent many years in India. It was only in the ninth century that the Chinese emperor cracked down on all foreign religions.

The leaders of St Thomas Christians repeat proudly that their pre-Latin Christianity is Indian in culture, Christian in religion and oriental in worship. These claims may be greatly justified *vis-à-vis* Latin Christianity, though the first Cardinal of the Syro-Malabar church did not hesitate to call it the 'zero-Malabar' church, reacting to certain trends in the community to revitalize the Syrian traditions in preference to Indianizing its liturgy. Curiously, some recent writers of the community have referred to the ethnic affinity between the Sumerians (Chaldeans) and the Dravidians (of South India). It is not clear if this argument is part of a logic aimed at dispelling the 'foreignness' of the Syrian connection! However, unlike the Syrian-Indian Christianity of early China which disappeared without any visible impact, the community in India has been manifesting an increasingly active missionary trend, extending itself over the Indian subcontinent and other countries of the community's diaspora. Nearly 70% of the missionary personnel in India is of the St Thomas Christian community, with eight eparchies in North India. The origin of the expansion is not very unlike early Christianity's connection with the Jewish diaspora worldwide, and its gradual liberation from its ethnic roots. This process of the cultural liberation of St Thomas Christianity and its unrestricted openness to other regional cultures of India has yet to manifest itself more firmly. Only a regional cultural leadership and hierarchy in the communities of Syrian rites and an effective check on the subtle process of Romanization that seems to be infiltrating its structures would mark a definite change in this direction and prepare the way for the emergence of an Indian rite with composite regional diversity. Both Syrian and Latin caricatures of Christ would then wither away.

The Latin Christ of the Western colonialists

The Portuguese arrived in India under pressure of navigational and oceanic trade developments that were threatening further to marginalize their newly-born country. The Portuguese bourgeoisie had succeeded in cleverly tapping the crusading spirit that had earlier enabled them to achieve national independence. This was a fight for national survival in an already glutted small internal market of Europe. It could be won only by breaking the monopolies of the Italian city-states who had worked out a mutually advantageous *modus vivendi* and *operandi* with the Muslims who had blocked Europe's breathing space eastwards since the seventh century. The Portuguese crown and nobility could mobilize its poor masses to sweat it out in the voyages of 'discovery' and the founding of an empire with the lure of wealth and with the hopes of eternal reward for their piety and sacrifices in defeating the 'enemies of the cross'! This was a piety of the Portuguese who at that time hardly knew any fragments of the biblical text correctly. It was a fundamentalist response to the Islamic fundamentalism that threatened their existence. It could not be expected that Portuguese coming from such a background and described by an outstanding Portuguese novelist Eça de Queiros as *'plebe beata, suja e feroz'*, that is, a fanatical, filthy and ferocious crowd (the rest of Europe was not much better in their small mediaeval world of the times) should understand the subtleties of the Hindu religion and philosophies. Further infected by the fanaticism of the Counter-Reformation in the 1540s, they yielded to a spree of temple-destruction and anti-Hindu legislation, making the living conditions of the non-converts socially and economically difficult, if not impossible, in their *Estado da India*. To claim that this was not 'violence', as many apologists of Portuguese missionary methods do, would mean arguing about violence against brute animals, not human persons. It was a triumphant Christ of the triumphant Western colonialists! Only some missionaries who hailed from the cosmopolitan city-states of Italy (unlike the missionaries of the nation-states of Europe) could manifest a cultural openness towards the Indians, Chinese and other non-European cultures.

In the process of this colonialist Christ-revelation the earlier Christ of St Thomas Christians was also doomed. He had already become a Christ tainted with the paganism of the native cultures, or more correctly a Christ who did not serve the economic-political interests of his Portuguese believers. This was a conflict that broke the unity of the St Thomas Christians in 1653 with their determination to resist Latinization with the oath of Koonan Cross. The Latinization through *Padroado* was aimed at chanelling the well-known military and commercial strengths of the St Thomas Christians of Malabar to the service of the Portuguese spice trade and empire. The struggle of the St Thomas Christians for identity is on, and it is hoped that they too will not forget, as the Latin rite Christians have often forgotten, that it is not by seeking self-identity and then by imposing it on others, but by losing it in incarnational solidarity with the oppressed and those with no self-identity, that Jesus was raised and proclaimed as Christ the Lord! A colonial Christ is thus a contradiction in terms, in which an *individual and unique* Christ is sought to be worshipped, forgetting that incarnation meant solidarity with all mankind and with creation.

The unbound Christ

Christ cannot be anyone's proud possession. He is an unbound Christ who has broken all the bonds and represents a God-experience beyond all names, a God-experience that many old spiritualists and religions of Asia and the world have aspired to, and not always in vain. God-experience should need no guises or disguises. Those who claim the power to bind in heaven what they bind on earth are probably also the ones of whom Jesus on the cross said that they do not know what they are doing and prayed for their forgiveness. He also warned: 'People will come from the east and the west, from the north and the south, and sit with me at the feast in the Kingdom of God. Then those who are now last will be first, and those who are now first will be last' (Luke 13.29–30), and: 'Not everyone who calls me "Lord, Lord" will enter the Kingdom of Heaven . . . I will say to them, "I never knew you, get away from me"' (Matt. 7.21–23).

Bibliographical Note

No footnotes have been provided in this paper because the author had to write it in circumstances which did not enable him to have access to any book material or notes. However, some of his own past writings and some of the other works mentioned hereafter may be usefully consulted for checking factual details or to help further reflection on the issues raised in this paper. The author acknowledges his debt to

George Soares-Prabhu in the form of some insights and bibliography which have been further developed here.

For a useful survey of contemporary approaches to christology, cf. J. A. Fitzmyer, *Scripture and Christology: A Statement of the Biblical Commission with Commentary*, New York, 1986. A useful discussion on recent New Testament christology can also be found in *Semeia* 30, 1985 and J. Sobrino, *Christology at the Crossroads*, New York and London 1978.

Walter Bauer, *Orthodoxy and Heresy in Earliest Christianity*, Philadelphia and London 1972, offers a classic description of the origins of 'orthodoxy' as representing the form of Christianity supported and actively propagated by the church of Rome, but never fully accepted elsewhere.

For more information on St Thomas Christians and for insights into the rites controversies in India the *Christian Orient* (published by CMI religious in Kerala since 1980) is very helpful. The works of A. M. Mundadan, especially his *Indian Christians Search for Identity and Struggle for Autonomy*, Bangalore 1984, provide somewhat more balanced views of the Syro-Malabar camp than do most other writers belonging to that Rite.

C. R. Boxer, *The Portuguese Seaborne Empire*, London 1977 and *The Church Militant and Iberian Expansion*, Baltimore 1978; *O Pai dos Cristãos* (=Father of Christians), ed. J. Wicki, Lisbon 1969; Teotonio R. de Souza, *Medieval Goa*, New Delhi 1979; and M. D. David (ed.), *Western Colonialism in Asia and Christianity*, Bombay 1988, contain some of the recent research on Portuguese and general colonial church attitudes in Asia.

II · The Non-Christian Perceptions of Christ

Hindu Perceptions of Christ in the Nineteenth Century

Samuel Rayan

Hindu perceptions of, and responses to, Jesus Christ in nineteenth-century India were as varied as Jewish perceptions of, and responses to him in first-century Palestine. They ranged from hostility and rejection, through shades of admiration, appreciation and friendship without commitment to his person and project, to total surrender to him in a community of disciples. Hindu perceptions are best seen as integral to the renaissance of Hinduism as well as to its resistance to new pressures and challenges. The factors that provoked and shaped the renaissance and the resistance also governed Hindu perceptions of Christ. At the basis of the ferment lies the old religion – the many-faced Hindu spiritual tradition with its relentless quest for the Absolute, its many ways of liberation, its general openness to other spiritualities, no less than its new awareness of unwholesome beliefs and practices which had come to infect it in the course of its long history. The new stirrings were provoked by Christian missionary activity; by the colonial presence of the West claiming to be a Christian power; by the introduction of Western education; by the work of orientalists who brought to light and made available to an élite public ancient India's immense religious and cultural riches; and by the rise of self-conscious nationalism, proud of India's history and heritage.

Types of perception

Some seven types of perception-response to Christ may be distinguished:

1. Christianity was seen by some as the religion of foreigners and conquerors, and Christ as an invader, a kind of religious Julius Caesar. Both were sensed as a threat to the traditional faith and to the nation's social

fabric. In response the old faith was reaffirmed and defended in all its forms and practices or in its scriptural essentials.

2. Others welcomed the Christ of the Sermon on the Mount, the ethical Christ, as against the Christ of metaphysical dogmas and mystical obfuscations.

3. There were others who recognized Jesus as an Asian and felt close to him. He was different from the denationalizing European Christ of the missionaries and of their warring denominations.

4. Christ as *the* incarnation was unacceptable to most Hindus, while Christ as *an* incarnation was welcome, especially to devotees of Vishnu. But every species of incarnation was repugnant to the theistic (deistic) outlook fostered by Islam and Western rationalism.

5. Others there were who worshipped Christ as Saviour, Son of God and God-Man. All this was understood differently from traditional Christian orthodoxy. This Christ was the centre of a new dispensation, a universal church harmonizing the religions of the world.

6. A few persons, however, after cherishing for a while one or more of the above positions, came finally to orthodox ecclesial faith in Christ as God's Word incarnate come to redeem the world.

7. There were those, too, who looked upon Christ as liberator from social and religious oppression. It was thus they knew him in some church or other, despite the presence of oppressive factors within the churches themselves.

It remains now to illustrate these different positions by briefly studying persons and movements, representative of one or another of the many trends indicated above.

Love, with reservations

Christ, the moral preceptor. Rammohan Roy (?1772–?1833)

In 1820 Rammohan Roy of Calcutta published *The Precepts of Jesus, The Guide to Peace and Happiness*. The volume contained extracts from the four Gospels, covering Jesus' teachings on right and holy living. For Rammohan, founder of an association called the Brahmosamaj (1828), religion was ethical existence. The moral law, partially taught by all religions, was principally inculcated by Christianity. He found the teaching of Christ admirably calculated to elevate people's minds and regulate their conduct. He separated the teaching of Jesus from the historical facts of Jesus' life, death and resurrection. These could be disputed by anti-Christians, and had little spiritual or theological significance. Jesus was a theist; his disciples misunderstood him; and the whole edifice of christology was a mistake.

Rammohan developed his view of Christ in controversy with a Serampore missionary, Marshman. Jesus was the Messiah, God's supreme messenger. He was son and servant of God, but not God, the Ruler of the universe. He receives everything from God, is dependent on him and subject to him. Jesus is the first-born of all creatures, produced in the beginning. He pre-existed in God's purposes for the whole of creation. The unity between Jesus and God is a unity of will and design. Rammohan rejected belief in the incarnation as idolatrous and polytheistic. The Christian view of Jesus's death as expiation for sin is rejected too. The idea of justice implied in the atonement is inadequate. Jesus has made it clear that pardon is available through repentance, and that mercy and justice are more acceptable to God than sacrifice.

Rammohan's view of Christ differs deeply from Christian faith. Still, the high esteem in which he held Christ, his admiration for Christ's incomparable greatness, his acknowledgement of the central role Jesus plays in God's saving work, the close connection he sensed between salvation and ethics, place him close to the mystery of Jesus Christ, which he would perhaps have discovered in full faith had his search not been diverted by being forced into an insightless, Western-style controversy.

Christ: divine humanity. Keshub Chunder Sen (1838–1884)

From 1857 onward Keshub was associated with the Brahmo Samaj and with its vicissitudes. Like Rammohan, he admired Jesus for his moral greatness, but he went farther to accept the person of Christ in his paschal mystery and his trinitarian relationships. Keshub's views on Christ found expression in the lectures he delivered between 1866 and 1883. Four of these lectures are particularly relevant and revealing: (i) Jesus Christ: Europe and Asia, 1866; (ii) Christ and Christianity, 1870; (iii) India asks, Who is Christ?, 1879; and (iv) That Marvellous Mystery – the Trinity, 1882. Beginning with the perception of Jesus as a great man and a reformer Keshub proceeded to recognize him as divine humanity, and went on to rehabilitate him as the second person of the Trinity, the universal Logos, incarnate Sonship.

In 1866 Keshub summed up the story of the spread and influence of Christianity, and concluded Jesus' 'extra-ordinary greatness and super-natural heroism'. He stressed the Asianness of Christ, regarded the Cross as a beautiful symbol of self-sacrifice, and reduced the resurrection to an experience the disciples had when their sinking spirits were roused by the noble self-sacrifice of martyred Stephen. Jesus meant love of God and love of man. 'By Christ I understand one who said, Thy will be done', and 'When I talk of Christ I mean simply the spirit of loyalty to God'. In 1879 he returns to the theme of the Asianness of Christ; Christ is oriental. But the focus of his attention is on the divinity of Christ, Christ's divine humanity. Christ emptied himself, and as the self ebbed away, heaven came pouring into his soul, divinity filled the void. Everything within him was divine. There, then, is the 'Christ before us as a transparent crystal reservoir in which are the waters of divine life'. It is thus Christ is the Son; he is made of Divine Humanity. He existed in God before he was created.

Keshub claimed that the doctrine of divine humanity was essentially a Hindu doctrine. Through the doctrine of absorption in the deity India will reach Christ, and Christ will fulfil the Hindu dispensation, including its error-stricken pantheism. For 'in Christ you see true pantheism', 'the union of the obedient and loving Son with the Father'. Christ comes to us as an Asian in race, a Hindu in faith, a kinsman and a brother, a true Yogi, full of sweet devotion and dwelling always in the supreme Spirit: 'My Christ, my sweet Christ, the brightest jewel of my heart, the necklace of my soul, – for twenty years have I cherished him in this way my miserable heart.'

By 1882 Keshub comes to contemplate Christ right within the mystery of the Trinity. The unspeakable Jehova-Brahman descends in his Son, an emanation from his self, touches and permeates the universe and humanity, and then draws up the regenerated world to himself in the power of the Holy Ghost. 'The Trinity of Christian theology corresponds strikingly with the Saccidananda (=Sat,Being; Cit,Mind; Ānanda,Bliss) of Hinduism. There is but one substance, one person, but 'three conditions, functions and manifestations mingling in synthetic unity'.

Christ is not man-God but God-man. 'Divinity is engrafted upon humanity', which remains integral. The resurrection is now rethought and understood as something that happened to Jesus. It means that Jesus returned to the Father with all his humanity. Christ is not the Father, but 'humanity pure and simple in which Divinity dwells'. 'He was the Father's begotten Son, a creature', co-eternal with the Father (!). He was, is, sonship incarnate, and his work is to teach sonship. The atonement, too, is accepted. 'In Christ's death more than in his life was the saving economy of providence fulfilled.' The Cross 'deluges the world with faith, hope and love' (Scott, 219–47 – for details of works cited see the end of this article).

Keshub synthesized and reconciled within himself Hindu and Christian traditions, giving rise to something new. This may have prevented him from identifying exclusively with either. He was more successful than most missionaries in establishing the spirit of Christ in India (Scott, 40). Keshub's richest religious experience came from Christ (Farquhar, 66f.).

Christ: sweet prophet, oriental and fascinating. Pratap Chander Mazoomdar (1840–1905)

Mazoomdar's perception of Christ is not very different from that of Keshub, his friend and colleague in the New Dispensation, a kind of church which sought to harmonize all spiritual traditions. His experience of Christ is reflected in his work *The Oriental Christ*, which carries thirteen meditations on the beauty, the holiness, the power of the sweet prophet of Nazareth. Christ is contemplated as he bathes, fasts, prays, dies and reigns. In dark and lonely days and spiritual wanderings Mazoomdar has sought and rejoiced to find pure, simple, strong manhood in Jesus. As a sense of sin and of restlessness grew on him, he was mysteriously led to feel a personal affinity to Christ, whose life and death had for him 'a marvellous sweetness and fascination'. Despite discouragement and ridicule, 'I persisted in according to Christ a tenderness of honour which arose in my heart unbidden' (7–10).

Mazoomdar's special concern is to 'orientalize' Christ. Jesus, presented in the garb of Western ideals and theologies, has failed to make contact with the distinctive 'spiritual instincts' of Hindus. The author portrays two contrasting figures of 'Christ' and concludes: 'When we speak of an Eastern Christ, we speak of the incarnation of unbounded love and grace; and when we speak of the Western Christ we speak of the incarnation of theology, formalism, ethical and physical force.' Let Christ be made recognizable and acceptable to all (42–46, 17–13).

Jesus is unique. He completes all other, partial and local, incarnations, and embodies the true, universal relationship between God and us. God's self-revelation in Christ has an ultimacy. Nature, history, incarnations, Jesus Christ: these are stages in the progressive unfolding of the Divine Spirit. Christ is the Spirit's perfect, unique, ultimate manifestation. Hence when Christ bathed, whole humanity bathed in him. We bathe daily in his baptism. But to purge and renew the very substance of our person, was not some other baptism necessary – the baptism of fire and the Spirit, the baptism of suffering and blood? That is what Jesus provided by devoting his fresh, young, pure life as a sacrifice (50–2).

Love going all the way

The three men we have met so far took their stand at the point of intersection of Hinduism, Christianity, liberal theology and rationalism. They followed Christ with caution and reserve. Others of the same elite renaissance group went all the way and joined a Christian church in the conviction that Christ was not perceptible apart from his community. Their view of Christ coincided in large measure with their church's.

Christ: cit and sacrifice. Brahmobandhav Upadhyaya (1861–1907)

Influenced by his uncle Kalicharan Banerjee, Christian and nationalist, Bhavanicharan was attracted to Jesus from early boyhood. In the Brahmo Samaj and its offshoots, this attraction was nurtured and clarified by Keshub's and Mazoomdar's devotion to Christ. As a teacher in Sind he began to be preoccupied with the theological status of Christ, and eventually publicly professed his faith in Jesus as perfectly divine and perfectly human. That was in 1890; the next year he got baptized and before long joined the Catholic church. In 1894 he became a Catholic ascetic and took the name Brahmobandhav. For him Christ is the centre, claiming attention and allegiance as the universal teacher, the revealer of the mystery of God's inner life, and God's Son able to undo the bondage of karma.

Brahmobandhav's interest focussed on the indigenization of the faith and the church. He finds Jesus prefigured in certain Vedic texts and the inner life of God 'foreglimpsed' in Indian scriptures (Lipner, xlvf.). After 1897 he shifted from Vedic theism to Vedantic Advaita as the best framework for Catholic theology, though when the question of incarnation and grace arose, it was to Vaishnavism that he appealed.

Christ: the inspiring cross. Narayan Vamana Tilak (1862–1919)

Brahmobandhav lived in Sind and Bengal, Tilak lived in Maharashtra, but they were kindred spirits. After his marriage at eighteen, Tilak spent ten years in many jobs and much wandering. Once in a train a man spoke to him of poetry and Christianity, prayed with him, and gave him a copy of the New Testament. Tilak was deeply moved by the Sermon on the Mount. In time he came to the conclusion that Christ was the teacher India needed. He felt drawn to Christ the ideal man who identified himself with the Father, and had an unfailing faith in himself as the light and life of the world. Christ combined the love of God and people in a single demand, and stirred everyone by his self-sacrifice. Baptized in 1895, Tilak taught religions and poetry, wrote patriotic and religious poetry, and worked to make the church truly Indian. He is said to have had a vision of Christ, and that led him to fuller renunciation and years of life in an ashram.

Christ: liberator. The depressed classes and dalits

The depressed classes of India, a sixth of the nation, a mass of crushed humanity, have been held down by Hindus at the bottom of society in ignorance and degradation. All hope of foreseeable betterment was cut off by the theory of karma and rebirth. Many of them began to see in missionary practice a way out of their wretchedness. They perceived the Christ of the mission as a liberator. In 1910 the Mahars of Maharashtra held a conference in Pune and drew up a memorial to the Secretary of State in which they described their crushed condition and appealed to British law to right the wrong. At one point they said that 'the kindly touch of the Christian religion elevates the Mahar once and for ever, socially as well as physically'. They were demanding that British justice do as much for them even as they continued in their ancestral faith. There we have a record of Mahar experience of liberation by Christ – a significant perception of Christ by outcastes. The document dates from 1910, but the events referred to belong in the nineteenth century.

Defence of Hinduism

Controversies

Hindu pandits had a long tradition of controversies and apologetics, as well as of dealing with religious pluralism. The nineteenth-century Hindu-Christian controversies were provoked by aggressive evangelism. The situation was met with a corresponding criticism of Christianity and a defence of Hinduism, sometimes reasoned and nuanced, sometimes assertive and total.

A debate and tract-battle was waged in the 1830s in the Bombay area. It was called forth by the criticism and contempt poured on Hindu Puranas by John Wilson (1804–1875), a Scottish presbyterian and Indologist. There were public debates in 1830 and 1831 in which it was asked, for instance, of what God Jesus was the son, how God could die, whether Jesus had no other way of saving us, how bread and spirit and water could bring holiness . . . A certain professor Narayana Rao entered the fray with Wilson and circulated a Sanskrit work, the title of which translates, 'One who takes Pride in his Country's Religion'. The work, following a literalistic exegesis, ridiculed a creator who needed rest, had the form of man, etc. If Christianity were true and necessary it should have existed from the beginning and been preached in Hindustan long ago (Young, 30–1).

Perhaps the most remarkable Hindu-Christian encounter was occasioned by the publication in 1839 of *Matapariksa* (An Examination of Religion) by John Muir, Scottish civil servant and orientalist. The work was 'an acerbic but sophisticated Christian treatise' in Sanskrit. It provoked three important critical replies: one in 1839 from Somanatha of central India; another in 1840 from Harachandra, a Calcutta pandit; and the third in 1844–45 from a Bararese pandit, Nilakantha Goreh. Soma's was irenic, Hara's blustering, and Goreh's systematic and severe. In all of them the assessment of Christianity is uniformly negative because Christianity's understanding of God, the world, humans and salvation differs from that of the Vedas which are the ultimate norm. A curious feature of the Hindu apologetics was the absence of Jesus Christ. The reason may be that Christ was not central in Muir's work. There the accent was on Christ's work as saviour. If the apologists had little to say about Christ, they had much to say about non-human life. Christianity's unconcern about that life was a graphic demonstration of the unsoundness of the Christian faith (Young, 137).

The Arya Samaj: back to the Vedas

The Samaj was founded by Mūla Sankara (1824–1883) in 1875 in Bombay. Mula Sankara, born in Kathiawar, became a wandering ascetic, got initiated as Dayananda Saraswati, and completed his *Satyaprakāsh* (The Light of Truth) in 1874. The purpose of the book and of the organization was to recall Hindus to their original religion as it is in the Vedas; to stir up opposition to non-indigenous religions like Islam and Christianity; to prevent cow-slaughter; and to purge Brahmanical religion of polytheism, image worship, animal sacrifice, belief in incarnation, etc. The central dogma was the infallibility of the Vedas. Around it was built belief in *karma*, rebirth, the sanctity of the cow and importance of sacramental rituals. Dayananda admitted that the Brahmo Samaj had saved a small number of Hindus from embracing Christianity, but he accused the Brahmos of imitating Christians in some things and admitting forgiveness of sins (Saarma, 164).

Ramakrishna Paramahamsa (1836–1886): Many paths to the same God

Ramakrishna's life represents the entire orbit of Hinduism. For Ramakrishna the many religions are branches of one tree, and paths to the same God. He has demonstrated this by practising the spiritual discipline of Yoga, Tantra, Bhakti, Advaita, Islam and Christianity. He was introduced to Christ by a non-Christian, Sambucharan Mallik (Jadu Nath Mallik), who had studied the scriptures of various religions and had chosen Jesus as his personal deity. One day in the garden house of Mallik,

Ramakrishna noticed a picture of the Madonna with the divine child. As he watched, it became animated and emitted a light which entered into him, pushing aside all his Hindu ideas. A deep regard for Christ filled his heart, and he entered a new realm of ecstasy.

Four days later he saw a beautiful serene figure coming to meet him. A voice in his heart assured him that this was the Christ who had suffered for humankind, the Master-Yogin, the embodiment of Love. 'Based on this vision Sri Ramakrishna maintained an intense devotion to Christ throughout the remainder of his life' (Stark 88). For him Christ was an incarnation of God, though not the only one. There were others – Buddha for instance and Krishna. And so Christianity was a path leading to God-realization. This view was but an integral part of his own tradition which therefore was defended and strengthened by his experience.

Vivekananda (1863–1902)

Born as Narendra Nath Datta and initiated to sanyasa as Swami Vivekananda, this great disciple of Ramakrishna inherited the master's devotion to Christ. His *Life* (1949) tells the story of how, after Ramakrishna's death, a dozen or so monks took their monastic vows on a Christmas Eve after invoking Christ's name and blessing under Vivekananda's leadership. The monks gathered before a fire for meditation. Naren began to tell the story of Jesus. Through his eloquence the boys were admitted into the world of Jesus and of Paul. Naren made his plea to them to realize God and to deny themselves 'as the Lord Jesus had done' (159–60).

Sister Nivedita testifies that Vivekananda considered himself 'servant of the servants of Jesus. Had he lived in the days of Jesus in Palestine, he would have washed Christ's feet not with his tears but with his blood' (276). *The Imitation of Christ* was one of the two books he carried with him during his monastic wanderings. But Vivekananda defended Hinduism against missionaries, and with his emergence Hinduism's new missionary outreach began. He proved 'a doughty champion of the despised religion' (Sarma, 294). In his view what India needed was not a new imported religion, but the uplift of its masses, the power of organization, and the strength the Vedanta teaches (282–83, 304).

Conclusion

The perceptions and responses are many and varied. Some of them were shaped by the image of Christ projected on the scene. It was often an image dimmed or distorted by its association with foreign conquest and colonial domination by people who professed to be followers of Christ. It was further warped by the aggressiveness of evangelism. Christianity and Christ were seen as forces at home with practices of oppression, greed and the violation of (other) people's dignity. They did not bind their votaries to justice and gentleness, nor did they care to raise a standard of protest against their infringement. Had the Christ of the Gospels been introduced to India in a context of equality and freedom, and had the meaning of the cross and the dimensions of love been presented in a different manner, more positively and respectfully, would there not have been a wider, deeper, more beautiful response?

That is not to suggest that with better missionary methods India's religions would have at once yielded to Christianity and vanished. The suggestion rather is that a larger and profounder dialogue would perhaps have taken place, leading to serious theological explorations into India's perennial claim that God has always provided for the salvation of all peoples, and of her repeated attempts at shaping a religion for humanity by harmonizing the finest experiences and perspectives in all spiritual traditions. There would then have emerged the Face of the One whom Keshub called the Greater Christ, the One Word who mediates all creation, all history of love and forgiveness and struggles for justice, and all sanctifying and energizing activity of the Spirit from end to end of time and space. Such a dialogue would have led us to discover the spiritual horizons within which to see the fact of religious plurality in perspective, and to understand the various symbol systems not only as many paths leading to God but as God's many ways of coming to us in our concrete historical situations, as so many signs of his presence, memorials of his voice heard, of his face seen as in a mirror, darkly.

A survey of nineteenth-century Hindu perceptions of responses to Christ invites us to a deeper and more comprehensive contemplation of the Christ who has always been in this land, and who goes before all missionaries and calls for finer sensitivity to his ways of coming and going and companioning.

The story in Luke 24 of a walk to Emmaus is the story of humankind. Sit down to break bread and news together in mutual hospitality, and recognitions will come of hidden lights and fires and of the hidden Master.

Bibliography

Andrews, C. F., *The Renaissance in India. Its Missionary Aspect*, London 1912.

Farquhar, J. N., *Modern Religious Movements in India*, London 1924.

Lipner, J., and Gispert-Sauch, G., *The Writings of Brahmabandhav Upadhyay*, Bangalore nd.

Mazoomdar, P. C., *The Oriental Christ*, Boston 1883.

————, *The Life and Teachings of Keshub Chunder Sen*, Calcutta 1887.

Nivedita, Sister, *The Master As I saw Him*, Calcutta, [10]1966.

Parekh, M. C., *Rajarshi Rammohun Roy*, Rajkot 1927.

————, *Brahmarshi Keshub Chunder Sen*, Rajkot 1931.

————, *A Hindu Portrait of Christ*, Rajkot 1953.

Sarma, D. S., *Studies in the Renaissance of Hinduism in the Nineteenth and Twentieth Centuries*, Benares 1944.

Scott, David C., *Keshub Chuner Sen. A Selection*, Madras 1979.

Stark, Claude Alan, *God of All. Sri Ramakrishna's Approach to Religious Plurality*, Massachussetts 1974.

Thomas M. M., *The Acknowledged Christ of the Indian Renaissance*, Madras [2]1976

The Life of Ramakrishna, Mayavati, Almora [6]1948.

Young, Richard Fox, *Resistant Hinduism. Sanskrit Sources on Anti-Christian Apologetics in Early Nineteenth Century India*, Vienna 1981.

Chinese Non-Christian Perceptions of Christ

Kwok Pui-lan

'Who do you say that I am?' This question was first posed by Jesus to his Jewish disciples. Later, when Paul and other evangelists preached the gospel to cities around the Mediterranean Sea, Gentiles of the Greco-Roman world were confronted with the same question. For centuries, the answers to the christological question were largely shaped by Christians living under the influences of Hebrew and Greek civilizations during the formative period of Christianity.

When missionaries introduced the gospel to Asia, the christological debate was rekindled in another cultural context, in the midst of the rich and diverse religious background of the Asians. Many Asian people have a linguistic structure, thought-pattern, world-view, and life-style that are radically different from the West. The Chinese, for example, continue to use a hieroglyphic form of writing, though other ancient civilizations had changed to other forms of writing long ago. They have also developed complex and intricate philosophies, oriental art-forms, and literary masterpieces based on that writing system.

Christianity was introduced to China first by the Nestorians in the seventh century, and later by Roman Catholic and Protestant missionaries. For scholars steeped in the Confucian tradition, Christianity was a foreign idiosyncratic teaching, a heterodoxy just like Buddhism and Daoism. For local gentries and officials, the missionaries threatened their leadership and prestige in the communities. In the early twentieth century, Christianity was vehemently criticized as both imperialistic and unscientific by young students and radical intellectuals during the anti-Christian movement. Since the seventeenth century, there appeared in China a sizeable amount of anti-Christian tracts, pamphlets and anthologies written by Confucian and Buddhist apologists. This body of widely circulated literature not only illustrates the conflicts between two cultures, but also provides ample resources for understanding Chinese non-Christians' perceptions of Christ.

Jesus as God incarnate

Before the missionaries could proclaim that Jesus was God incarnate, they had to find a Chinese term for 'God'. For more than three centuries, the missionaries and the Chinese could not settle the debate over how to render the Hebrew and Greek terms *Elohim* and *Theos*, or God, into the Chinese language. The translatability of the term 'God' epitomizes the differences that exist between Chinese and Indo-European languages. But the difference in language only reflects the deeper divergence in mental categories and thought-processes.[1] The missionaries believed there is a supreme being, who creates and rules the universe, and God is the name for this 'self-existent, eternal, almighty Being, the Creator of heaven and earth'.[2] In contrast, the Chinese conceive of cosmogony as a dynamic, continuous and organismic process in which there is no creator who stands outside the universe.

The French Sinologist Jacques Gernet explains why it is difficult for the Chinese to conceive the notion of being, in the sense of an eternal and transcendent reality, beyond the phenomenal world. He writes: 'There is no word to denote existence in Chinese, nothing to convey the concept of being or existence, which in Greek is so conveniently expressed by the noun *ousia* or the neuter *to on*. The lack of these concepts or mental categories does not suggest essential inferiority, but rather different modalities of thought.'[3]

Since the Chinese do not conceive ultimate reality in the substantive language of 'being', they find it extremely difficult to entertain the thought that God would assume corporal substance or exist in human form. Many authors of anti-Christian literature emphasized this point. For example, a writer in the seventeenth century asked:

> Does this great governor of the universe who created everything have a corporal substance? If he does, who created him and where was he before Heaven and Earth existed? If he has no corporal substance he is what our Confucianism calls Taiji (the cosmic origin). But the Taiji can have neither love nor hatred. And how could it demand that people obey it? How could it dispense rewards and punishment? . . . But there is worse to come: they claim that the Master of Heaven descended to be born on earth as a man . . . So where was he before he descended?[4]

For most non-Christian Chinese, the idea that Jesus is the incarnation of God in history was simply implausible and irrational. Given the fact that Jesus was only born in the West Han dynasty in the long civilization of China, they had reason to doubt where God was in the many preceding dynasties.

Other Chinese, who were more familiar with Buddhist teachings, found certain similarities between the notion of incarnation and the transformed body of the Buddha. The Buddhists believed that the Buddha existed in the form of the spiritual body and also in the body of transformation. Some even felt that Christianity had plagiarized certain tenets of Buddhism. However, there were also basic differences. First, since Buddhism regards phenomenal existence as illusion, the incarnation of God could only be an unreal manifestation. This would be comparable to the heresy of Docetism in the early church. Secondly, Buddhism believes that the body of transformation of the Buddha manifests in hundreds and thousands of people. The non-dualistic Buddhist thinking holds both the 'one' and the 'many' together. In sharp contrast, Christianity insists that God was manifested on an unique historical occasion, in the person of Jesus.[5]

The Jesus of history

If the Chinese could not quite understand how Jesus could be God, many also found the extraordinary events in Jesus' life hard to believe. Since the Chinese paid a lot of attention to a person's family background, they were interested in knowing more about the parents of Jesus. The gospel stories did not provide much information about Jesus' ancestry, and his miraculous birth from a virgin sounded strange not only to the Chinese, but also to their Western contemporaries influenced by the Enlightenment.

One Chinese *literatus*, writing in the mid-nineteenth century, stated that Jesus was born out of wedlock, a view widely held by those Chinese embittered by the opening of the Chinese hinterland to the missionaries in the 1860s:

> Jesus was born in Judaea. His mother Mary, who was not yet married, blasphemously said she had a child from God. In fact, Jesus was a person without a father . . . (As recorded in Western sources, Mary was a virgin when Jesus was born. But Jesus had an elder brother. Giving birth to a son without a husband was really the custom. It was not only Jesus who had no father.)[6]

Jesus' low social status as an illegitimate child was compounded by the fact that he associated with people of lower class and doubtful origins. Confucius, the Chinese sage, had seventy intelligent students, and the great neo-Confucian scholar Zhu Xi opened an academy for the *literati*. Jesus, in contrast, had tax-collectors and fishermen as his disciples. Furthermore, many Chinese were amazed that one of his disciples who had followed him for several years finally betrayed him.

Judged by the Confucian standard, Jesus was far from being a praiseworthy son who showed filial piety toward his parents. Referring to the passage in which Jesus said that whoever does the will of God was his brother and mother (Mark 3.32–35), some Chinese writers criticized that Jesus did not even recognize and respect his own mother. Jesus' followers were also accused of not observing the Confucian teachings regarding loyalty and filial piety in their human relationships.

In Chinese folk religions, stories of miraculous healing and recovery abound. The fact that Jesus performed miracles to heal the sick was considered as one more proof that Christianity, like these folk religions, was a heterodox teaching meant for the ignorant masses. In Christian apologetic, Jesus' ability to heal the sick is interpreted as a sign that Jesus is the Son of God. But in the Chinese mind-set, this ability is nothing special, since many famous Chinese medical doctors and healers were believed to have the power to save people from death. In the early twentieth century, when science became almost like a 'religion' for the radical intellectuals, the miracle stories were seen as 'relics of the past', challenged by both historical studies and science.

Many Chinese harboured unsettling doubts about the Gospel stories of Jesus' death and resurrection. One famous Chinese *literatus* of the nineteenth century, Yu Zhengxie, questioned whether Jesus' death was caused by the crucifixion. He asked: 'If Jesus had really been put to death on a cross, how could (his followers) bear to treasure the object on which he was so cruelly punished, and revere it so highly?'[7] But most other writers believed that Jesus was indeed crucified, a proof that he was a criminal condemned by the Roman authority. Like the people who mocked at Jesus when he was crucified, the Chinese could not believe that the man nailed on the cross could be the saviour of humankind. Yang Guangxian, an orthodox Confucian in the seventeenth century, who believed that Christianity was a menace to the Chinese way of life, remarked: 'Not only was Yesu (Jesus) not able to save mankind as a whole, but he himself was sentenced to the most ignominious of deaths. Could this be the Master who created heaven? His bid for power has failed, he did not submit quietly to justice but prayed to Heaven on his knees . . .'[8]

Jesus' resurrection was considered to be utterly inconceivable by the rational Confucians, who insisted that Jesus' body was stolen by his disciples. Having secretly done that, the disciples spread the rumours that Jesus was resurrected after the third day. But the Buddhists, with richer religious imagination, could recast the story of resurrection in their own terminologies, as one missionary lamented: 'Use whatever language you please to express the resurrection, and the uninitiated will understand it to mean transmigration.'[9]

Jesus as teacher

Although the non-Christian Chinese were generally unimpressed by the life of the historical Jesus, they had quite diverse views about his teachings. The average Chinese would be more comfortable with the image of Jesus as a teacher of the Western people, just as Confucius and Mencius were their great teachers. Some could even admit that there might be good things in Jesus' teaching to be assimilated by the Chinese. Such tolerant attitudes were partly the result of respect shown to the early Catholic missionaries, who in turn were ardent students of Chinese classics.

Clad in a Confucian robe, the great Jesuit missionary Matteo Ricci spent years learning the Chinese classics. In his important theological treatise, *The True Meaning of the Master of Heaven*, Ricci unavoidably used Chinese terms and idioms and employed Chinese concepts to communicate Christian thought. Some of the *literati* would have thought the teachings of the Master of Heaven were not so radically different from that of the Chinese. Since the Neo-Confucian scholars had also assimilated many concepts and ideas from Buddhism, there might be a genuine possibility of synthesizing Confucianism with Christianity. Ricci's disciple, the scholar-official Xu Guangqi, preached a kind of amalgamation of Confucianism and Christianity among his colleagues.

But the more positive attitude towards the teaching of the Master of Heaven did not continue long, as other Catholic friars from the Dominican and Franciscan orders did not adopt such an open and inclusive stance towards Confucianism. The bitter Rites Controversy resulted in the expulsion of the missionaries and the condemnation of Christianity as heterodoxy by the Chinese Emperor in 1724.

Hostility towards Christianity mounted as missionaries were finally allowed to preach the gospel in China as a result of unequal treaties signed between China and Britain and France in the mid-nineteenth century. After repeated humiliation by the West, Chinese intellectuals realized that the foreigners, with their warships and cannon balls, and their strange religion, presented a real threat to China. Zeng Guofan, the famous scholar-official who helped in suppressing the Taipings, and who blended Christian teachings with Chinese folk religions, warned that if Chinese were to accept Christianity, the result would be:

> Scholars would not be able to study the Confucian classics, which are different from the so-called teaching of Jesus, the New Testament. The thousand-year-old Chinese rites, ethics, poetry, history, laws and institutions would be totally destroyed in one day . . . Our Confucius and Mencius would be crying bitterly in their graves.[10]

The view of Zeng was shared by other contemporary Confucian scholars. In the anti-Christian literature written during this period, the authors emphasized that the teachings of Jesus would undermine the five relationships in Chinese society because Christians believe that all people are brothers and sisters. Christianity was accused of subverting the social relationships, encouraging sexual impropriety, and even advocating the domination of women over men.[11]

In the early decades of the twentieth century, Chinese intellectuals were more open to Western thoughts and institutions, as they were looking for ways to save China. However, many believed that China had to adopt science and democracy from the West, but not the Christian religion. The anti-Christian writings of Zhu Zhixin, a leader of the Guomindang, was widely circulated. In an essay entitled 'What is Jesus?', Zhu questioned the character and teaching of Jesus. Referring to the parable of the ten virgins in Matthew 25, Zhu asked how those five girls who came prepared could be admitted to the Kingdom since they were selfish and did not even offer help to their friends in need. The cursing of the fig tree in Mark 11 was also seen as revealing the vengeful character of Jesus.[12]

But a contrasting view was presented by Chen Duxiu, who became one of the early leaders of the Chinese Communist Party. In an important essay 'Christianity and the Chinese People', published in 1920, Chen spoke highly of the person of Jesus, although he dismissed the theories of creation and Trinity as incredible. For Chen, the character and teaching of Jesus could contribute to the moral regeneration of the Chinese people. If the Chinese could emulate the noble character and fervent emotion of Jesus, Chen said, they could be saved from the pit of darkness, filth and coldness. Chen also emphasized Jesus' teaching of forgiveness, sacrifice and universal love as important for the Chinese.[13] Like Chen, many liberal Chinese Christians also believed that Christianity had the potential to save China because it could be a force for moral regeneration.[14]

Jesus as the redeemer

In the christological debate in China, the most controversial issue was the Christian affirmation that Jesus is the redeemer of humankind. Christianity believes in the depravity of all human beings, and Augustine's interpretation of original sin influenced the Western understanding of humankind for centuries. Since human beings are sinners, they can only be reconciled with God through the death and sacrifice of Jesus the Christ.

The humanistic Confucian tradition understands human nature and propensities very differently. Both Confucius and Mencius emphasized the potentialities in human nature for good rather than for evil. Through learning the Chinese classics, self-cultivation, and developing one's moral faculty, there is a genuine possibility for human beings to achieve moral perfection and sagehood. This general optimism in human nature is shared by Mahayana Buddhism, which emphasizes the capacity of attaining Buddhahood in all human beings, and the possibility of sudden enlightenment.[15] Many scholars have insisted that there is no equivalent concept of 'sin', understood as fundamental depravity in a religious sense, in classical Chinese culture. The Chinese speak of shame and guilt rather than 'sin'.

There have been many different atonement theories in the West, trying to provide answers to the difficult question: how can Jesus be the saviour of humankind? These theories invariably borrow metaphors and concepts from human experience, and they are clearly culturally bound. For example, the ransom theory was based on the Roman penal system, and the expiation theory clearly bore the marks of the sacrificial rituals of the Jews. Some of these theories might not be easily understood by people of the modern West, not to mention by the Chinese with a different mental framework. Concerning the ransom theory, one man of letters states:

> They say that the Master of Heaven paid in person for the crimes of the ten thousand generations. That is totally incomprehensible. Since the Master of Heaven is majesty without equal and infinite compassion, why did he not simply issue an amnesty to men for their crimes, and what need had he to redeem their crimes with his own person? . . . And if he was capable of redeeming the crimes of men with his own person, why was he not capable of arranging that men should commit no more crimes?[16]

To make the theory of atonement more accessible to the populace, missionaries found that they could borrow religious terminologies and concepts from Chinese folk religions. Folk Buddhism believes that the merits (*gongde*) of ancestors, immortals and bodhisattvas can be computed to future generations. In the religious tracts and Christian catechism, many missionaries explained that Jesus, as our mediator, bore our punishment, and his merits can be computed to our names. But many Confucian intellectuals did not have much regard for these folk religions, and some questioned the fairness in computing merits in this way:

> If suddenly a minister of great merit were to memorialize requesting that he alone be blamed and that there be no punishment of the crimes of the thousands who had revolted, on the ground that his merit was sufficient to equalize (their crime), would this be right?[17]

Even if the merits of Jesus could be transferable to us, he is not the only saviour, for there are other Buddhas and bodhisattvas. Growing up in a pluralistic context, many Chinese found it offensive that they had to believe in a foreign saviour with an exclusive claim for their salvation.

The above discussion illustrates that it is often difficult to communicate philosophical and religious ideas in a cross-cultural context. In the past, the response of the Chinese towards Christianity has been generally negative because the missionaries and even many Chinese Christians insisted that they had to accept the Western interpretation of the life and work of Christ. Even today, Christianity is seen as a 'foreign religion' by the majority of the Chinese. Instead of requiring the Chinese to accept christological answers formulated by another culture, it might be worthwhile understanding more sympathetically the non-Christians' perceptions of Christ. This kind of cross-cultural study poses new questions to our hidden presuppositions, and opens new avenues for us to ponder the significance of Christ in our religiously pluralistic world.

The Chinese non-Christians' perceptions of Christ has also changed over time. Their receptivity to Christ depended on how well they could fit the christological puzzle into their Chinese framework, and to what extent this picture of Christ could address the needs of China at the time. Antiforeignism and strong nationalism have prevented many Chinese from developing a more genuine understanding of Christ. In contemporary China, where many people lose their confidence in Marxism, a growing number of young intellectuals are attracted to Christianity. As the Chinese struggle for democracy and human rights, some intellectuals are beginning to look into the religious roots underlying Western democracy and come up with a more favourable reassessment of Christianity. We hope a more meaningful encounter between Christianity and the Chinese people can be possible in the near future.

Notes

1. For a discussion on the 'term question' from a feminist perspective, see P. L. Kwok, *Chinese Women and Christianity, 1860–1927*, Atlanta, Georgia 1992, 31–8.

2. W. J. Boone, 'An Essay on the Proper Rendering of the Words *Elohim* and *Theos* into the Chinese Language', *Chinese Repository* 17, 1848, 50.

3. J. Gernet, *China and the Christian Impact: A Conflict of Cultures*, Cambridge 1985, 241f.

4. 'Tianxue chuzheng', in *Pixie ji* (c. 1643), quoted in Gernet, *China* (n. 3), 221.

5. See Gernet, *China* (n. 3), 229.

6. 'Shang xiekui Wo Liangfeng shangtang shu' (1863), in *Fan yangjiao shuwen jietie xuan* (Selected Anti-Christian Writings and Memorials), ed. M. L. Wang, Jinan, Shandong 1984, 24.

7. See P. A. Cohen, *China and Christianity: The Missionary Movement and the Growth of Chinese Antiforeignism*, Cambridge, Mass. 1963, 38.

8. Quoted in Gernet, *China* (n. 3), 228.

9. Signed by C., 'In What Form Shall We Give the Bible to the Chinese?', *Chinese Recorder*, 21, 1890, 454.

10. 'Tao Yuefei xi', quoted in *Jindai Zhongguo yu Jidujiao lunwen ji* (Collected Essays on Modern China and Christianity), ed. Z. P. Lin, Taibei 1981, 21.

11. 'Tianzhujiao xieji', in *Pixie jishi* (A Record of Facts to Ward Off Heterodoxy), 1871, 2–3.

12. Zhu Zhixin, 'What is Jesus?', in *Chinese Essays on Religion and Faith*, ed. D. Lancashire, San Francisco 1981, 230–3.

13. Chen Duxiu, 'Christianity and the Chinese People', 211–12.

14. W. H. Lam, *Chinese Theology in Construction*, Pasadena, Ca 1983.

15. J. Ching, 'Confucianism: A Philosophy of Man', in *China and Christianity: Historical and Future Encounters*, ed. J. D. Whitehead *et.al*, Notre Dame, Indiana 1979, 8–28.

16. Quoted in Gernet, *China* (n. 3), 226.

17. Quoted in Cohen, *China* (n. 7), 53.

Does Christ Have a Place in Asia?
A Panoramic View

Aloysius Pieris

This article attempts to spell out what could be the response of a committed and reflective minority of Asian Christians to the question posed above.

Obviously, the question has to be split further: which Christ and why? Here, one has to sort out the various 'Christs' claiming Asia's allegiance, specifically,

> the *Euro-ecclesiastical Christ* of the official church;
> the *non-Western Christ* of scholars and intellectuals; and
> the *Asian Christ*.

History's response to our initial question, however, is harsh and clear: *they are all out of place in Asia*, but each for a different reason. History being a reliable teacher, I have allowed its verdict to set the agenda for my investigation.

Asia has always been impenetrable to Christianity (a mere 3% converted after two millennia). This was not necessarily or primarily due to Christ's colonial appearance; nor, conversely, would an indigenized Christ have tricked the Asians to accept Christianity. In Part I and II, I cast a doubt on these assumptions, in order to isolate the real issue for our discussion in Parts III and IV.

I The Euro-ecclesiastical Christ of the official church

Riding on the waves of colonialism, the Euro-ecclesiastical Christ swept to power in Latin America as he did a little later in the non-Islamicized tribes of Africa, and continues to do so in Oceania. Why, then, did he fail to capture Asia, except in a few well-definied areas? Let me reiterate, here, a plausible interpretation of this strange phenomenon.[1]

My explanation presupposes two types of religiosity: the *cosmic* and the *metacosmic*. The former embraces all tribal and clanic cultures whose religiosity consists of revering nature and its forces, either in the form of a numinal being or a numinal complex of beings who is/are, nevertheless, so much part of the world as to be encountered in the context of an ecological spirituality. Animism is a pejorative misnomer for it. The cult of the spirits and cosmic forces, such as the Bons (Tibet), Devas (S. Asia), Nats (Burma), Phis (Thailand, Laos, Cambodia), spirits of ancestors (Confucianist cultures in Korea, China, Vietnam), Kamis (Shintoist Japan), etc., are constitutive elements of this religiosity.

The *metacosmic* refers to the so-called great religions which posit the 'existence' of an immanently transcendental horizon (Brahman-Atman, Nirvana, Dao, etc. in the 'gnostic' religions; Yhwh of Moses, Abba of Jesus and Allah of Muhammad in the three 'agapeic' religions), Which/Who is salvifically encountered by humans, through liberating knowledge (*gnosis*) and redemptive love (*agape*) respectively.

The mechanism involved in the rejection of Christ in Asia can be explained by what can be facetiously called 'the helicopter theory of religious expansion'. The theory is based on four historical observations:

(*a*) The first is that the metacosmic religions are like helicopters, while the cosmic religions serve them as the natural landing-pads. Their encounter is one of mutual fulfilment, as they are complementary. Hence there is no radical conversion from one to the other. Thus, 'inculturation' means none other than a metacosmic religion finding its natural point of insertion in a cosmic religion. This is how all non-Christian religions spread in various parts of Asia. The spread of Christianity in the Philippines, as also in Africa and Latin America, seems to have followed the same pattern.

(*b*) The second trend seems to be 'First come, first served'. Buddhism has come to Thailand before Christianity. Christianity has come to the Philippines in those areas where no other metacosmic religion has preceded it. That is why Thailand is Buddhist and the Philippines are Christian, today. Tantric Hinduism in Java was of a cosmic type, and Islam did not find it too difficult to penetrate its culture.

(*c*) Thirdly, it is usually the case that once a helicopter has landed, another cannot land on the same pad. This means, for example, that the Philippines will not become a Buddhist country, just as Thailand will not be Christian. In other words, *mass conversions from one metacosmic religion to the other is improbable*. Only where a cosmic religiosity still prevails (e.g. Oceania and certain pockets of Laos and Cambodia and the tribal regions of India, as well as certain parts of Korea where Buddhism is more Confucianist than metacosmic) is there evidence of a Christian break-through. In certain parts of Indonesia (North Sumatra, Ambonia, Moluccas) Christianity had won (a few millions of) converts, probably because a cosmic religiosity had a stronger sway over the masses than did Islam. The rest of Asia would not let Christianity sweep across its religious cultures.

(*d*) Fourthly, the possibility of a helicopter being *forced out* of its landing pad is not ruled out. A metacosmic religion could replace another by exerting prolonged and persistent political or military pressure or even through demographic changes (i.e. through migratory colonization). The history of religions in Central and West Asia abounds in examples of this.

These four trends, by no means absolute, but indicating a historically observed pattern of religious expansion, explain why colonial Christianity did not strike roots in most parts of Asia. It is not necessarily the colonialness of Christ that is rejected, for we see his Euro-ecclesiastical figure being successfully enthroned in cosmic cultures that are being Christianized today. In fact, *Redemptoris Missio* singles out Asia as a field for a quantitative expansion of Christianity (37). 'Open the doors to Christ!', it appeals (3). But our prognosis based on the observations made above is that the cultures that have absorbed the great religions – that is over 90% of Asia – have no room for Christ except perhaps as one cosmic power among many, i.e. as one more deity in the pantheon of cosmic forces, rather than as the one Lord and Saviour.

II The non-Western Christ of intellectuals

Our focus, here, is mainly on attempts made by some Christians or groups of Christians to break out of the existing theological moulds in order to communicate the Christ-event in the context of the *other* Asian religions and cultures. Let us reflect on four such attempts, two in China and two in India.

The first in our list is the 'Buddhist Christ', so to say, of the Nestorian community which flourished in China from 635 to 845 CE. Judging from extant records,[2] we could call their experiment 'inreligionization' as distinct from inculturation.[3] The latter, as I explained above, is the unchallenged entry of a metacosmic religion into the ethos of a cosmic religion. But in the Nestorian experiment, we see a metacosmic religion (Christianity) developing a new Asian identity within the idiom and the ethos of another metacosmic religion (Buddhism) – something that falls outside the general pattern observed above (Part I).

Thus, for the first time the Christian soteriology had been reformulated within the Buddhist world-view, while the Avalokitesvara/Kuan-Yin model had served to form a 'Buddhist christology'.[4] To appreciate the bold originality of this experiment, one must contrast it with the syncretism of the third-century Manichaeans who concealed the person of Jesus in a forest of Buddhist terms and concepts.[5]

Obviously, in other parts of Asia the Nestorians had different experiences, and the documents of their headquarters in Mesopotamia witness to both dialogical and hostile attitudes towards Buddhism.[6] At any rate, if the 'Buddhist Christ' of the Chinese Nestorian communities did not last more than about two centuries, it was not because of any ecclesiastical intervention, but because of Emperor Wozong's ruthless suppression, in 845 CE, of all so-called 'foreign religions' – which included both Buddhism and Christianity.

Hence we have no way of ascertaining how far the 'Buddhist Christ' of the Nestorian scholars would have appealed to the Chinese masses. We can only conjecture that Nestorian christology and the monastic witness of that community might have contributed much to the emergence of this 'Buddhist Christ' who, nevertheless, remains dead and buried in the writings and inscriptions of the past.

The second breakthrough came a millennium later with Matteo Ricci entering China. Rejecting Buddhism as incompatible with Christianity, he built on the cosmic religiosity of Confucianism, thus opting for inculturation rather than inreligionization, as we now see retrospectively.

His becoming a Mandarin scholar in China is paralleled by Roberto de Nobili's becoming a Brahmin Sanyasi in South India. Both these men made many converts and established Christian communities. Here, it is the misunderstandings within the church that saw the end of such efforts. Had they not been suppressed, what would be the fate of such communities today in Red China with its anti-Confucianist socialism or in modern India with its growingly anti-Brahmanic self-assertion of Dalits (about whom, see below)?

As for Red China, where Ricci is still not without honour, we know that the Patriotic Church did look for a Christ having a Sino-ecclesial expression within the framework of anti-Confucianist socialism,[7] whereas the Underground Church repudiated such attempts as a treacherous compromise with an atheistic ideology and confessed their adherence to Christ in conformity with their inherited ecclesiastical mode of relating to the Western churches. The universal church waits anxiously to see how the Chinese Christians will resolve this conflict and what kind of Christ will emerge from their reconciliation, and what place such a Christ will occupy in this gigantic segment of Asia. In the present article, therefore, this case is left out of our critical evaluation.

In India, too, there were new developments. As De Nobili's work faded into history, there emerged another figure of Christ, the 'Gnostic Christ' of the nineteenth-century Hindu Renaissance: a God-man, in whom the divine and the human enjoyed moral (rather than an ontological) unity, perhaps a Christ severed from his ecclesial body, but familiar with the idiom of metacosmic Hinduism.

Significantly, however, this Christ emerged mostly from the pens of well-meaning Hindu and Christian scholars of the so-called high castes. Obviously the Hindu masses would not have been aware of these attempts, nor did all of the Hindu elite welcome the new incarnation,[8] while the church as a whole was reluctant to absorb this trend. One wonders whether this Indian Christ of the nineteenth and early twentieth century survives today outside the historical treatises that deal with that epoch.

To sum up: none of these four Christs has found a place in the hearts of the masses, nor in the minds of the majority of today's elite. The reason in each case differs, as explained above.

As for the authenticity of these 'Christs', however, we have two ways of making an assessment: one would be to embark on a long and laborious analysis of the christological worth of these creations; the other – this is what I propose to do – would be to place them side by side with the *Asian Christ*.

III The Asian Christ

The Asian Christ is my shorthand for the 'Christ of Asia' whom the Asian bishops addressed in their liturgy at their pan-Asian conference of 1974. But my focus here is not so much on the 'Asianness' of this Christ as on the 'Christness' of those categories of Asians who alone can reveal his Asian features. This emphasis has guided me in selecting *four* such categories for discussion.

(a) The Broken Body of the Indian Christ

The humiliations of India's *Broken Christ* have been woven, since the 1970s, into what is known as *Dalit Theology*.[9] 'Dalit' means broken, trampled upon, destroyed . . . obviously by the nefarious system of discrimination between the so-called high, low and scheduled castes, in India.[10] Their weak self-identity as untouchables and outcasts is derived from centuries of cruel *segregation* in matters of habitation, education, marriage, meals, burial, access to water and even to temples, and from a deep-seated socio-religious *stigma* of being a polluted and a pollutant species of non-persons. Since the 1970s all backward castes, tribals and landless labourers who maintain the primary sector of service in contemporary India, seem to have gradually earned the name 'Dalit'.

Mahatma Gandhi's condescending term *Harijan* (God's People) appeared offensive to the enlightened sections among them; they refused to be co-opted by the oppressive caste-system prescribed by the Hindu Canon Law (Dharma Sastras) which Gandhi adamantly defended as a sacrosanct and inviolable part of Hindu religion. Dalits prefer to be called what they have always been: Dalits, a broken people. (This brokenness presumably also includes numerous caste divisions and conflicts among the Dalits themselves!¹¹) Their stance is clear: their brokenness rather than their Christianness remains their identity, and consequently, also the basis of their Christo-praxis.

Hence, in the Dalit perspective, the Gnostic Christ was only a phantom which the Hinduizing Christians created while treading on the body of this authentic Indian Christ. Those great pioneering indigenizers¹² now face trial before the Dalits. Even Christian Ashrams that dialogue with Hinduism's metacosmic religiosity, without ever allowing the broken Christ to utter a word of challenge, are a party to this sin against the Body of the Lord! The Third World theologians, too, have been severely criticized for speaking of the Indian poor in general without singling out the scandalous plight of the Dalits even within the church.¹³ For the great majority (in some areas 60%, in others almost 90%) of Christians are claimed to be Dalits, but 90% of church leadership and the theological industry is alleged to be in the hands of a minority of 'upper-caste' Christians! The broken Christ has no place even in the church, which, therefore, could not be the body of *that* Christ!

Many Dalit theologians reject *in toto* the Marxist tools of social analysis so dear to some 'Third World Theologians' of India. For not only did the Indian Marxists fail to grasp caste structure – most of them were from the 'upper' castes, and had no first-hand experience of the Dalit reality – but Marx's own theories about Indian society and its prospective liberation relied too blindly on indologists like Max Müller and on the administrative reports of British colonizers who did not have an inside knowledge of caste-infested rural India.

Thus, in Dalit theology, the Exodus text dear to the liberation theologians yields place to the confessional formula of Israel's historical roots: Deut. 26.5–12. Since Dalitness is the constitutive dimension of their theology, the broken Christ whom they identify themselves with, follow behind and minister to, is for the most part non-Christian! Hence, their participation in the Dalit Movement in general is an essential part of their christopraxis.

Since it is not only in civil society but also in Christian communities that the Dalit Christ is refused a place, the struggle is both against the Euro-ecclesiastical Christ of the official church and against the Hindu Christ of Ashramites, both of whom fear the consequences of abdicating their place in favour of the Broken Christ. An official option on the part of certain groups (religious congregations) to 'go Dalit' in ministry and even in their recruitment is rumoured. If it is true, the Indian church will soon climb the cross where it will be fragmented before being gathered into a Christ that India aspires for.

(b) The han-ridden body of the Korean Christ

In the Minjung Theology of Korea,[14] this same Asian Christ appears with a 'han-ridden body'. 'Han' is a mixture of many things: a sense of *resignation* to inevitable oppression, *indignation* at the oppressor's inhumanity, *anger* with oneself for being caught up in that hopeless situation . . . and a host of other emotions which are all accumulated to form a powerful source of psychological energy possessing a revolutionary potential if released in a socially organized fashion. In day-to-day life, this revolutionary energy is released in small doses through rite and ritual with the aid of Shamans. But the most dramatic release of *han* is the mask dance in which *prophetic humour* is exercised by the Minjung (the oppressed people) against the Confucianist elite and the monastics (of metacosmic religion which, in Korea, is Buddhism) who side with the oppressive system. It is a symbolic enactment of the Minjung's unconcealed aspiration for freedom.

A distinction is made between *daejung*, the (confused) masses, and *minjung*, the (conscientized) people.[15] Does it not imply two moments in the life of the Korean Christ: the *han*-ridden moment and the *han*-releasing moment of the messianic people? Does not the passage from one to the other constitute the Korean christopraxis?

This brand of Asian theology emerged in its present form only in the 1970s, in the words and deeds of imprisoned and/or tortured farmers, workers, students, professors and journalists, who discovered their prophetic role by a *reditus ad fontes*, a return to the ancient (non-Christian) Korean sources of liberation: the *minjung* tradition. *Minjung* theology was a theological appropriation of a *minjung* Christianity which, in its turn, was a Christian appropriation of the (non-Christian) *minjung* tradition.

The Christianization of the *minjung* tradition occurred in the nineteenth century in a way that marks out Korea as the first Asian country to sow the seed of a theology of liberation. For the first time, an Asian nation received the Bible, not as the aggressive foreigners' holy book – for Korea's colonizer was Shinto-Buddhist Japan, and not the Christian West – but as a sacred history of the *minjung*. Japanese and Chinese being the languages of the Korean literati, the appearance of the Bible in Korean language (and in the Hangul script) had an explosive effect on the *minjung*. Here was a God in solidarity with the *minjung*, announcing the word of liberation in their own despised language and through their own folk idiom of narrative, drama and poem, so different from the abstract jargon used by the God of missionary catechesis!

From its inception, therefore, Koran Christianity was a politicized faith and played a significant role in the national liberation struggle, unlike in other Asian countries, where it was the non-Christian religions that stirred nationalist sentiments against Western colonizers. No wonder that the books of Exodus and Daniel were banned in Korea as potentially subversive! Whence we draw this conclusion: *the Bible, when made accessible to the oppressed in Asia, easily becomes the seed of an authentically Asian Christianity, as it allows the best of Asia's (non-Christian) liberative traditions to be absorbed into the church's conscience*. No wonder that there was a concerted effort by pastors to depoliticize and privatize the faith of Korean Christians, and not without success.

Even today, collusion between the neo-colonialist Christianity and developmentalist ideology conspires to keep the unshepherded masses (*daejung*) from leaving their chains and exercising their role as a messianic people (*minjung*). The Passover from the *han*-ridden state of the Suffering Servant to the *han*-releasing hour of exaltation is the only way for the Asian Christ to manifest himself in Korea as the covenant between God and the oppressed. What hinders this Korean christophany is the perverse order of Mammon, which reserves a place only for a Christ without a cross, a Christianity which is comfortable with that disorder.

(c) The breast-feeding Christa of Asian womanhood

Asian women have no place, even where they wear themselves out at the service of males: in homes, and offices; fields, forests and factories; tourists' resorts and night clubs; and, of course, temples and churches. Their Christhood has been powerfully captured by Hyung Kyun Chung in her wood-cut painting of the 'Korean Christa': an open-armed Shaman-woman stretched on a cross and mounted on a lotus, with a sword in one hand and a bowl of rice in the other; the pierced side of the Crucified One issuing the waters of the Spirit is depicted in the form of an exposed (female) breast ever available for suck.

This image emphasizes the fact that a woman-shaman does not occupy a reputable place in society but remains the most accessible source of consolation and comfort for the *han*-ridden masses of women. She is the 'priest of *han*'.[16] Extending this observation to all cosmic religions of Asia, Chung notes:

> The existence of women-defined popular religiosity in Asia, such as Korean Shamanism, folk Chinese Buddhism which venerates Kwan In (female goddess), Filippino worship of Ina (mother-god), is powerful evidence of women's resistance to patriarchal religions.[17]

Here one might add South Asia's Kali, Pattini, and other female manifestations of divine justice, to whom the poor and helpless appeal against their oppressors.[18]

Note that all these cults belong to the cosmic level of the great Asian religions. For all metacosmic religions condone or even commend patriarchalism in their Holy Writ and in their traditions. Like casteism, sexism, too, is a religious and not merely a socio-economic oppression. Often, not always, it is at the cosmic end of the Asian religious spectrum (popular religiosity) that women discover religious symbols to protest directly or indirectly against their servile state, or create some space for themselves even within religion.

The cosmic approach to feminism differs from the secularist one. The latter reflects the anti-religion of feminists reacting against the anti-feminism of religion. But the 'cosmic' is a blend of the earthly, the womanly and the religiousness of the poor. The involvement of women from the oppressed classes in ecological movements,[19] therefore, is a distinctive feature in Asian feminism.

Hence in Asia there is a tendency to appropriate theologically what was once condemned as 'popular' (and in my vocabulary, 'cosmic') religiosity. For it is the religiosity of all the four categories of the Asian poor mentioned here. It is the spirituality of the Asian Christ among whose members discrimination in terms of 'male and female, high-caste and low-caste, or Christian and non-Christian' (Gal. 3.28 !) is less accentuated than among those who refuse him a place.

(d) The Third World Christ of Asia

The continuous use of the phrase 'Third World' irritates people who think it has lost its meaning since the collapse of the Second World. This is because they take the term 'third' to mean 'no. 3' in a numerical series, whereas in its original (French) usage it designated 'something different' from both the First and the Second World, a 'third way' of organizing society, an 'alternative' to the two existing models – a meaning that inspired the non-aligned movement.[20] Secondly, it also means the 'two-thirds world', the teeming masses of the destitute who form the vast majority in our planet. Further, it includes the idea that this world of the poor is in reality the waste product of a plutocracy led by the First World.

To these three meanings, the Afro-Asian and Latin American theologians add a fourth 'biblico-christological' significance: 'Third World' stands for the humble of the earth whom God has elected as the covenant partner in God's project of human liberation. It is also the Christ in whom Jesus continues as in his own members; through, with and in him alone the church is called to re-live its mission and *thereby* recreate its ecclesial identity.

The starving children of Jacob, who turned westwards to wealthy Egypt in quest of economic aid only to become the donor country's political and cultural slaves, were chosen by Yahweh to create a 'third way' of being a community in a land that significantly stood between Egypt and Babylon, the two super-powers of that time. Understandably, therefore, the Third World, summoned to partner Yahweh in building the new dream-world of justice and love, has now become a theological and even a christological challenge, in that the majority members of the body of the Third World Christ are both *Asian and non-Christian*.

IV The Asian Christ: a sign of contradiction

Asian theologies evolve in a dialectical process of resolving several conflicts, four of which are singled out below. Asian Christians need both time and freedom to resolve these conflicts in their own way.

(a) The three Christs in conflict

In traditional christology (through which I can make the Asian quest intelligible to the rest of the church) 'Christ' is a compendious title which has absorbed all that we believers have attributed to Jesus ever since the Easter experience. The elements crucial for our purposes are three: the name of Christ overlapping with the name of *the Trinity* (God's salvific presence in history) as in the earliest Asian (Syriac) anaphoras; Christ the Risen Jesus bound to his earthly body, *the church*, as in the Pauline catechesis; Christ as the continuity of Jesus' history on earth in the lives and struggles of *the poor and the dispossessed* who, as victims of human neglect, are also the eschatological judge of nations (Matthew 25.36 ff.).

Thus the preponderantly 'non-Christian' character of Christ has become a determinative factor in the four brands of Asian theologies explained in Part III. This poses no problem if we abide by the traditional belief that though all of Jesus is Christ, not all of Christ is Jesus (*Jesus est totus Christus, non totum Christi*). Jesus cannot grow to the full stature of Christ unless all his members (most of whom are non-Christians) together with the cosmos struggle like him, even unto death, in ushering in God's reign on earth.

The Christian members of basic human communities operate on this christology in the light of which the three images of Christ discussed above (see Part I) are subject to the following verdict:

Christ of the official church is not only European but also *ecclesiastical*; i.e., a clumsy body that hides its head which is Jesus. But the non-European Christ of the Asian élite suffers from the other extreme of not being *ecclesial*; it is a head minus the body, a Jesus truncated from the total Christ. In contrast to both these, the Asian Christ (as recognized, announced and served in the basic human communities) – at times called the non-Christian Christ – is the *true body*, even if it has not yet named its head.

(b) Two missiologies in conflict

Understandably, therefore, the Asian theological quest involves two conflicting missiologies, reflecting the three images of Christ. The one defines mission as somehow or other *procuring a place for Christ in Asia*; the other spells out the missiological consequences of recognizing and proclaiming *Christ as the one who has no place in Asia*.

The Euro-ecclesiastical Christ was just beginning to fade out of Asia thanks to the post-conciliar development of the theology of the local church, when the mission to Christianize Asia was somewhat de-emphasized in favour of the mission to Asianize Christianity. Some Asian churches, refusing to be a mere extension of the Western Patriarchate, strove to be for *all* Asians a readable sign and an accessible means of God's reign experienced in Asia from time immemorial.

Now, christology is the first casualty of this new ecclesiology, while proselytism is the second! For the 'Christ of Asia' that the Asian bishops addressed in their liturgy at their pan-Asian conference of 1974 seemed to have been in Asia *long before* the church arrived there, and at work even today *far beyond* the church. Were they all aware of their tacit acknowledgment of the 'non-Christian Christ' and his claims over the Asian church? The christological reflections accompanying the new ecclesiology was breeding missiological confusion and much apprehension in the church.[21]

Redemptoris Missio is an attempt to confirm these fears rather than to allay them. Despite reiterating many a conciliar teaching, it reveals its hidden agenda in the introductory paragraphs. One gets the impression that the church which has lost its grip on the secularized West would like to gain control of the religious South which is fast growing to be the new centre of Christianity in both numerical and qualitative terms, besides being the traditional arena of global conflicts. Alluding presumably to the sixteenth-century missions to Asia and the Americas, which helped to renew church life in Europe, the redactors of the encyclical want missionary zeal to be whipped up again in terms of the *plantatio ecclesiae* model of mission which, I suspect, guarantees a quantitative expansion of the Western Patriarchate's ecclesiastical control in the Third World.

The encyclical warns against placing the emphasis on the 'Reign of God' rather than on the church as the primary goal of mission. The mission is to expand the church; to get Asia to 'open the doors to [the Euro-ecclesiastical] Christ'! It is the missiology of creating a place for Christ everywhere in Asia. Some Asian scholar-theologians, as indicated above, have been equally irrelevant. They have endeavoured to *invent* a non-Western Christ that would have a 'respectable place' in the minds of the religious élite, rather than *discover* the Christhood of the Asian poor who, like Jesus, have no decent place to be born in (Luke 2.7), no reputable place to live and work in (John 1.46), no safe place in their own country to hide from oppressive rulers (Matt. 2. 13–14) or no honourable place to die in (Luke 23.23) and no place of their own to be buried in (Matt. 27.59).

(c) Two ministries in conflict

Hence it is the discovery of the Christhood of Asia's placeless and religious (mostly non-Christian) poor that has inspired a new theological quest along the second line of missiology mentioned above. Its goal is not to provide a place for the displaced Christ, but to be ministerially involved with him.

Now, in this ministerial praxis, too, we note two trends. One group exercises *the church's healing ministry towards the Asian Christ*. The other group seeks to participate in *the prophetic ministry that the Asian Christ exercises towards the church and society*. The former trend is represented not only by Mother Teresa and her sisters, but by countless other men and especially women, whose heroic charity is all the more Christian for being done without the public media advertising it at the expense of the poor. They work within church structures.

But the other species of ministry can succeed only in the basic human communities operating on the periphery of the official church. It is a mission which promises no consolation of the type that the first group enjoys. It is a massive plunge of faith into the project of human liberation and social transformation, based on the belief that the Asian Christ's placelessness in Asia is constitutive of the sin that infects both the evil and the religious society (including the church).

That is why the Asian Christ does not plead for a place in this sinful system; for he is its victim-judge, not an accomplice. The Christian mission, as articulated in the basic human communities, demands a conversion of Asian societies to Christ's order. Baptism is not a convenient mechanism to expand the church at the expense of the Asian Christ. It consists of 'making disciples of nations' (Matt. 28.19) along the *via crucis* of greedless sharing so that the life of each nation will be radically re-ordered in terms of the demands made by the Asian Christ.

The separation of these two ministries is an obstacle to the coming of God's Reign. The healing ministry can only serve to perpetuate the sinful order if the Asian Christ is not prophetically announced in word and deed as God's judgment over nations (Mother Teresa, pay attention!). But the prophetic activity of basic human communities can lead to ideological grooves through despair, unless healing miracles illuminate their word of liberation with a spark of hope, i.e., with glimpses into eschatological wholeness. The reconciliation of these two groups is crucial for another purpose which the Asian Christ demands: the re-evangelization of the official church by the basic human communities, something that requires the mediation of ministers of healing who operate within the church structures. Hence my final observation.

(d) The centre-periphery conflict

The official church, because of its minority complex, has often compromised its evangelical mission by its alliance with the ruling class, running institutions that produce the élite. Alienated from the Asian Christ, it may indirectly contribute to his placelessness. The official church's apostolic authority depends on its continuity with Jesus of Nazareth; but this continuity is strained if the church is not one continuous body with the Asian Christ. The basic human communities provide the channel through which it can re-establish this link and regain its lost authority, thus also loosening the chains of Euro-ecclesiastical feudalism.

For, in basic human communities the story of Jesus is appropriated as an Asian drama of liberation. The Christian members (though a minority in the basic human communities) retell this story as the story of the Asian Christ, declaring in word and deed, in liturgy and life, that 'Jesus of Nazareth whom they follow is the living Christ whom they serve here in

Asia'. The hierarchical centre of the church is the first addressee of this 'new evangelization' taking place on the periphery!

But such conversion at the centre, as I observed, is difficult unless the two ministries (the healing ministry *to* the Asian Christ and the prophetic ministry *of* the Asian Christ) merge into one christopraxis.

If that happens, the Asian Christ, a rock that God has placed for the church to stumble and fall on, may begin to serve as the rock of its salvation (see Rom. 9.32–33). Then the church will not waste its energy 'trying to procure a place for Christ in Asian societies'; it will rather wear itself out in 'transforming Asian societies that have no place for Christ'.

Notes

1. A. Pieris, *Asian Theology of Liberation*, New York 1988, 71–74 and 98–100.

2. E.g. the catechetical writings of Alopen, a Nestorian missionary who arrived from Mesopotamia in 635 CE, and also of Ching Ching (or Adam, to use his Christian name), as well as in the well-known stele erected in 781 CE by Yazedbouzid (Ching Ching's father), whose family came from Balkh, a Buddhist stronghold.

3. Pieris, *Asian Theology* (n. 1), 52.

4. For a neat summary with references, see David Scott, 'Christian References to Buddhism in Pre-Medieval Times', *Numen* XXXII/1, July 1985, 88–100.

5 See Hans-J. Limkeit, 'Jesus' Entry into Parinirvana: Manichean Identity in Buddhist Central Asia', *Numen* XXXIII/2, January 1986, 224 ff.

6. Scott, 'Christian References' (n. 4), 91.

7. For a very concise analysis of this attempt, see Frank K. Flinn, 'Prophetic Christianity and the Future of China', in J. K. Hadden and A. Shupe (eds.), *Prophetic Religion and Politics*, New York 1984, 307–28.

8. See Richard F. Young, *Resistent Hinduism: Sanskrit Sources on Anti-Christian Apologetics in Early Nineteenth-Century India*, Vienna 1981, 137–8.

9. My two main sources are: M. E. Prabhakar (ed.), *Towards a Dalit Theology*, Delhi 1989, and Arvind P. Nirmal, *A Reader in Dalit Theology*, Madras 1991.

10. The words 'high castes' and 'low castes' have now been replaced with the less odious 'forward castes' and 'backward castes' in contemporary Indian literature.

11. See Ghanshyam Sha, 'Dalit Movement and the Search for Identity', *Social Action* 40/4, December 1990, 217–35.

12. E.g. Upadhyay, Sundar Singh, Nehemia Gore, Krishna Pillai, Appasamy, Norman Vaman Tilak, Chencia, Chakkarai, to name the major figures, were all from forward castes!

13. However, it must be recorded here that at the Delhi Meeting of the Ecumenical Association of the Third World Theologians (EATWOT) in 1981, a hearing of the Dalit case was a major item in the exposure programme. In my input at that meeting (now Chapter 8 of *Asian Theology of Liberation* cited in note 1 above), I made a case for the Dalit and tribal struggle for liberation as a more important element for an Asian theology than the over-emphasized Hindu Renaissance.

14. The main source on which I base my reflections is: AA.VV., *Minjung Theology. People as Subjects of History* (1981), Revised Edition, New York 1983.

15. Kwon Jin-Kwan, 'Minjung Theology and Its Future Task for People's Movement', *CTC Bulletin* (CCA Hong Kong), 2 and 3, May-December 1991, 16–22.

16. Chung Hyun Kyung, *Struggle To Be The Sun Again: Introducing Asian Women's Theology*, New York and London 1990, 66.

17. Ibid., 112.

18. At the time of writing, the mothers of children who have disappeared in torture chambers in Sri Lanka are reported to be gathering frequently in shrines dedicated to these goddesses, demanding justice and seeking liberation from their pain.

19. See Gabriele Dietrich, *Women's Movement in India: Conceptual and Religious Reflections*, Bangalore 1988, 129–201.

20. See my 'Three Inadequacies in the Social Encyclicals', a paper read at *The Asian Seminar on the Future of Catholic Social Thought*, Hong Kong, March 1992, about to go to press.

21. See Felipe Gomez, 'Uniqueness and Universality of Christ', *East Asian Pastoral Review* 1983/1, 4–30, and Aloysius Pieris, 'Christology in Asia: A Reply to Felipe Gomez', *Voices from the Third World* XI/2, December 1989, 155–72.

III · Concrete Examples

Images of Jesus Christ in the Asian Pastoral Context

An Interpretation of Documents from the Federation of Asian Bishops' Conferences

Felix Wilfred

Settling down to write this article, the first thing I did was to look for the word 'Christ' in the index of the recently published collection of documents from the Federation of Asian Bishops' Conferences (=FABC).[1] To my surprise there was no such entry![2] This is already indicative of the fact that the bishops of Asia[3] have not *ex professo* dwelt on Jesus Christ, much less have they developed any christology. The documents are the statements of pastors, and the problems which occupy their attention are primarily of an ecclesiological nature. Whatever they have to say about Jesus Christ is occasioned, conditioned by and interwoven with their pastoral concerns.

The present article is an attempt to interpret the overall christological vision of FABC that underlies its pastoral pronouncements.[4] It is an *interpretation*, and not a string of quotations from FABC texts. The interpretation, however, is based on a close study of the texts themselves and my own experience of having assisted as a theological expert at two Plenary Assemblies and numerous consultations of FABC.

The Relevance of Jesus Christ for Asia

Every document of the Federation reflects a vibrant sensitivity of the bishops to the realities of Asia with which they are confronted. There is practically no document which does not start from, or at least include, some analysis of the Asian context. And the most striking characteristic of the situation is the *massive poverty*. Asia harbours several nations which are among the most impoverished in the world.[5] For the bishops, the relevance of Jesus is not a matter of theory and ideas; it is something immediately related to their experience of the negations and deprivations people suffer in this continent.

Jesus is relevant to Asia, not because the bulk of the Asian masses are *non-Christians*, but because they are *poor*. In fact, there is an inextricable relationship between Jesus and the poor. His message has a direct bearing on the poor who are called 'blessed'; it is to them the Kingdom of God is promised (Luke 6.20; 4.18–21). And therefore his message, his identifica-tion and solidarity with the oppressed and downtrodden, cannot but evoke ready response among the peoples of Asia. In the masses of Asia, marked by poverty, the bishops see the presence of Jesus; in their struggles and groanings, they perceive the paschal mystery of Jesus being re-enacted; in their powerlessness they see a 'liberating potential for spirituality', and recognize that the 'Gospel of the Kingdom is being shaped in the reality of their lives and the Spirit of Jesus the liberator is at work among them'.[6]

In effect, how relevant Jesus is in Asia will depend on the community of his disciples – the church – and the extent it makes the cause of Asia's poor its own.[7] Hence from the very beginning the bishops spoke about the church in Asia becoming a *'Church of the poor'*,[8] and declared in their First Plenary Assembly that 'dialogue with the poor' was a chief ingredient of their programmatic manifesto.[9] Here the model and inspiration for the church is the *kenosis*, the self-emptying of Jesus. The theme of the *kenosis of the church* after the example of Jesus is something that runs through the whole corpus of FABC documents; the bishops comment on this with remarkable consistency and insistence. This is so because it is of crucial importance for the *being* of the church in the midst of the Asian poor as the sacrament of Jesus Christ.[10] There is a further reason: the *kenosis* puts us in the right attitude in our relationships with neighbours of other faiths, and helps us to see without prejudice the universal plan of God.[11] It is this which will also lead us to work jointly with our brothers and sisters of other faiths 'to make the Kingdom of God more visibly present in Asia'.[12]

The legacy of the expansion of Christianity in colonial times has been its alien nature on Asian soil. And now the bishops see a new opening, a fresh opportunity for the entry of Jesus into Asia. They see Jesus as responding to the aspirations of the Asian masses. And these aspirations of the Asian poor are very concrete; it is a question of recovering their human dignity, their selfhood as persons. The poverty imposed upon them denies freedom to grow as full human persons and as communities. Jesus can make a relevant re-entry into Asia in this post-colonial period through a church that is humble and powerless, that is poor, that is in solidarity with the marginalized, sharing their lot.[13] This is a conviction very much ingrained in the reflections of the bishops.

The centrality of Jesus Christ and the universality of his message

The documents affirm unambiguously the centrality of Christ for our faith and for our Christian life.[14] He is the source, the inspiration and model of spirituality for believers. The bishops exhort intimate union with the person of Jesus and his mystery. But when this faith unfolds itself in the Asian context, it flowers concretely as the recognition of the universality of the message of Jesus Christ. Jesus is central for Asia because his spirit, his life, is catholic, universal, open to all peoples. His message of the Kingdom of God is the expression of the universality his person embodies. In seeking to respond to the challenges of the Asian context, the Kingdom of God becomes, in the thought of the bishops, a focal point.[15] It offers the most suitable framework for making sense of their two major experiences, which are also their chief concerns: the cultural and religious plurality of the Asian peoples, and the prevalence of massive poverty.

The connection they establish between the centrality of Jesus and the universality of his message can also be seen from the following fact: in trying to relate their faith in Jesus Christ and the situation of Asia, the bishops, in keeping with Vatican II (which in turn follows the teaching of early Christian writers), speak of the 'seeds of God's Word'.[16] But subsequently, faced with the concrete experiences and pastoral situations, they make the connection in terms of the 'seeds of the Kingdom',[17] which is a contextual and historical explicitation of the somewhat abstract 'seeds of God's Word'.

Lest there be any confusion, it is important, I think, to clarify the orientation of FABC to some current Western preoccupations about the relationship between Jesus Christ, the church and the Kingdom. It would be a total misunderstanding of the position of FABC if anyone were to think that it is trying to drive a wedge between the person of Jesus and the message of the Kingdom to highlight the latter at the expense of the former. At the same time its perspective and emphasis clearly differ from the concerns expressed in some Western circles. It is said in these circles that the *Kingdom* cannot be separated from the person of Jesus. The emphasis of the Asian bishops is that *Jesus* cannot be separated from his central message of the Kingdom of God. Jesus points to the Kingdom of God, and the Kingdom points back to the preaching of Jesus. The universality of Jesus' message of the Kingdom of God is not only pastorally the most viable approach in Asia, but it is also the key through which Asia can interpret the person of Jesus Christ.

Similarly, the bishops do not in any way try to underplay the place of the church by highlighting the Kingdom of God. Rather they focus attention on the church by reminding it of its serious *obligations* and onerous *responsibility* as a community called to follow the footsteps of Jesus.

Avoiding exclusivist and absolutist language

The Asian bishops are able to uphold the centrality of Jesus and the universality of his message without having recourse to absolutist language. In general the documents show a tendency to avoid exclusivist language. This is the result of the Federation's theological orientation.

First of all, the bishops' starting point is the universal plan of God's salvation for the world. It is within this framework that they understand the mystery of the person of Jesus Christ and his mission. This point is to be noted in view of some more recent missiological trends which start off from Jesus Christ. In this sense, the Asian bishops' orientation is in keeping with the conciliar document *Ad Gentes*.[18]

Secondly, they are keenly aware of the role of the Spirit in the economy of salvation,[19] and they try to see and interpret the historical event of Jesus Christ as having taken place through the power of the Spirit (Spirit christology). Thirdly, a dominant motif in the FABC thought is that of *pilgrimage*, *journey*. In keeping with the spirit of *Nostra Aetate*, which spoke of the common origin and destiny for the whole of humanity,[20] the Asian bishops frequently give expression to the fact that we are on a pilgrimage with all the peoples of Asia with their different cultures and religious traditions. This state of pilgrimage is the horizon against which we need to understand the mystery of Jesus and its proclamation. In short, the language of the bishops is not an absolutist or exclusivist but a *relational language* (which is not the same as relative): the mystery of Jesus Christ is in relationship with the overall plan of God, with the Spirit who is at work in the world, and with the neighbours of other faiths in Asia with whom we are united in a common journey. That leads us to the next point.

A distinctive Asian mode of proclaiming Jesus Christ

The bishops speak about the urgency of proclamation. But there is a distinctive way of understanding and practising proclamation: it derives from the Asian context to which church needs to respond in terms of dialogue, inculturation and liberation.[21] Speaking in general about mission, they acknowledge the interrelatedness of mission and dialogue, but also care to note that these are distinct, so that dialogue does not become simply an instrument of proclamation. However, mission, while having its own identity, cannot but be affected in its mode by dialogue.[22]

In this light, proclamation in Asia will differ because we are led to a deeper understanding of and growth into the mystery of what we proclaim through our relationships with neighbours of other faiths. Asia is not a *tabula rasa*. It has its own spiritual landscape against which and in interaction with which our faith in Jesus Christ can shine, and our proclamation can be meaningful and relevant. Because of this distinctive mode, when Asian bishops speak of proclamation, it should not be read and interpreted in terms of an ahistorical universal missiology, but must be understood in context.[23] In fact, the bishops rarely speak in terms of the classical sequence of proclamation, conversion, baptism and membership of the church. Their orientation is: proclamation, witness, Christlike deeds, dialogue, liberation, etc. In other words, proclamation is interpreted in terms of witness, dialogue and liberation, without exhausting it in these. For the bishops do recognize a role for oral proclamation. However, they see the source of it in the Spirit himself who will suggest when, where and how to do it.[24] Thus, reflecting on the basis of their pastoral concerns, the bishops have contributed to the growth of a distinctly Asian missiological tradition.[25]

The distinctiveness of Asian proclamation of Jesus Christ also derives from other factors. In the past there have been encounters of Asia with Jesus Christ and his message. The person of Jesus is admired and loved today by millions of Asians who are 'non-Christians'. And there are others who, while committed to Jesus Christ, for serious social reasons are not able to be members of the visible church. Facts and problems such as these have led the Federation to raise an important issue: to what extent is sacramental baptism related to commitment to Jesus Christ? This question was raised in the Institute for Missionary Apostolate (BIMA II), in the Bishops' Institute for Religious Affairs (BIRA II) and in the International Mission Congress held in Manila in 1979.[26] All that the bishops have done is to open up this question for reflection, without presuming to give any adequate answer at this moment.

Incarnation of Jesus and the local church

It is in the concrete, in the particular, that we really experience the validity of the universal. Jesus manifested his Christhood by deeply immersing himself in the world of Palestine, in a definite historical point, in a specific socio-political situation. It is this immersion of Jesus, his sharp sensitivity to what was happening around him, his passionate love for the least and the last, and his response to the challenges of the society and history of his times, that make us understand what incarnation really means. The ultimate mark of his total identification with his contextual particularity was his self-emptying in death. It is from out of this immersion in the particularity to the point of total self-giving that Jesus rose to become the universal Christ, the life-giving spirit.

Asian bishops are seized by the splendour of this mystery of incarnation. More than any other, it is this mystery which animates their thought and pastoral praxis. In the immersion of Jesus and his interaction with the society of his times, the bishops see the paradigm for their own mission in today's Asian society. For them, the universality of Jesus Christ is thus no abstraction, but something whose validity is attested in his response to the particular, to the concrete. It is this mystery of incarnation which really becomes the pivotal point for their understanding of the local church. To be a local church is simply to be Christlike here and today in Asia, discerning the signs of the times, and responding vibrantly to the call of God coming through the history, through the realities of our experience.[27]

In the conciliar and post-conciliar period, the idea of local church was brought to the fore, and much renewal and reform was centred on it. Attempts were made to identify the elements that constitute a local church, and especially to study the relationship between the local church and the universal church. Even now discussions continue about whether the local church comes first, or whether the universal church has priority, etc.

The theme of the local church as it figures in the thought of Asian bishops has a different focus and emphasis. The reflections of the Federation do not directly bear upon the above cluster of issues and problems. The Federation sees the local church, rather, from the perspective of Jesus' incarnation and mission in context.[28] The particular identity of the Asian church is shaped and the process of inculturation is set in motion when the community of the disciples of Jesus effectively responds to the challenges of the Asian situation.

The mystery of incarnation also provides another dimension to the process of building up the local church: there was growth in Jesus' wisdom and understanding (cf. Luke 6.20), a process in which the *milieu* of his life certainly had a significant role to play. The local churches of Asia are not only called to respond to the situation; they should allow themselves to be shaped by the Asian environment. This would make a concrete difference to the identity of the Asian local churches, for example, with the pervasive presence of peoples of other faiths in their environment.

Beyond inclusivism and pluralism

The religiously pluralist environment in which the Asian churches live raises the important question of Jesus and his universal mediation of salvation. This is so because daily experience shows our neighbours to be committed to their faith in other mediators, love and attachment to whom are reflected in their spiritual strength and ethical conduct. Hence the question of the relationship between our faith in Jesus Christ and that of our neighbours of other religious traditions.

Categories such as inclusivism and pluralism are used in the current discussion of the issue.[29] If the position of Vatican II in this regard can be characterized as inclusivism, so too can that of the Asian bishops in the early years of FABC. However, there has been an evolution in the thought of the bishops. Greater experimental and existential relationship with the faith of peoples of other faiths seem to have led the bishops a step further than inclusivism. This is what the spirit and cumulative evidence of the documents would suggest,[30] even though the bishops have not gone deeply into this issue. On the other hand, the bishops do not subscribe to a multiplicity of theophanies and divine mediations, each one independent in its own religious universe and equally valid. So we could say that the position of the Asian bishops is neither inclusivism nor pluralism. It seems to break these conventional categories and call for a new frame of interpretation.

Looking ahead

The Asian bishops have broached issues of great importance for pastoral praxis. They base themselves on their faith in Jesus Christ and derive inspiration specially from the mystery of incarnation. However, in order to achieve the pastoral goals and orientations they envisage, an Asian reinterpretation of Jesus Christ is very necessary. This has not yet been done. Evidently, we do not expect a full-fledged Asian christological interpretation from FABC, given its pastoral purpose. However, one could expect greater use of Asian resources in this regard – past and present. In fact, there is a rich tradition of attempts to reinterpret Jesus Christ in Asia. Thus for example in South Asia he is seen as *guru*, as *avatar*, as *satyagrahi* (one who is firmly planted in truth), as *jivanmukta* (the realized one), etc.[31] A christological reinterpretation will furnish a solid basis for the practice of inculturation in Asia.

In keeping with the Asian spiritual tradition, the bishops have attached great importance to prayer, contemplation, etc. A whole Plenary Assembly (Calcutta 1978) was dedicated to the theme of prayer. Asian Christian thinkers have found the Gospel of St John closer to the spirit of Asia, and have been fascinated by the image of Jesus presented in it.[32] The rich symbolism and interiority and the mystical dimension with which the Johannine image of Jesus is presented could be helpful to the bishops for a relevant pastoral praxis in this Asian continent.

I think that it is only when the bishops begin pastorally to confront certain important, but hitherto unexplored, issues and questions that the christological reflections of the Federation can go deeper. By way of example let me name some such issues which have not been fully addressed by the bishops, but which contain great potential for the development of relevant images of Jesus in Asia. First of all there is the fact of the millions of followers of Jesus Christ in Asia who do not belong to the visible church. Thousands of such people frequent our churches, assist at our religious services, and visit our shrines and pilgrimage centres. Many of them claim to have experienced Jesus Christ in their lives, and others have tried to interpret him. These experiences and interpretations could be of great value. Secondly, there is the pressing question of *women*. Unfortunately, the Federation has not really faced this issue. The experience of Asian women, discriminated against by traditional society and ruthlessly exploited by modernity, offers perspectives which can take us deeper into the mystery of Jesus Christ and to the heart of his message. Thirdly, there is the issue of religious fundamentalism in Asia, with its serious social consequences: violence, destruction and death. One of the reasons for this is the conflict of claims to absoluteness among the various religious traditions. In this context of general fundamentalism, for an appropriate pastoral praxis it is very important to rethink the traditional Christian language of presenting Jesus Christ, his person and message in Asia.

Conclusion

The Asian bishops have tried to relate our Christian faith in Jesus Christ to the challenges posed by the Asian situation in a creative way. This has led them to interpret proclamation in a distinctive way in the Asian world, and understand local church after the model of the incarnation of Jesus. Unfortunately, however, today a *restoration missiology* from outside is trying to penetrate into Asia, winning local satellite adherents. It judges the situation rather simplistically and from a distance, and mistakenly believes the the bishops have only spoken about dialogue, liberation, inculturation, etc., and have neglected the proclamation of Jesus Christ. This restoration missiology is causing regrettable disruption in the harmonious growth and evolution of the thought of the Federation. It is to be hoped that this importing of pre-Vatican and dated missiology into Asia is only a passing phenomenon and that in future the Federation will continue to follow the trajectory its abundant documents already indicate, and in the process contribute to the emergence of fresh images of Jesus congenial to Asia.

Finally, I am reminded of the story of a priest, very zealous and active in the charismatic movement. He put up a large poster on the wall of his parish church which read 'Jesus is the answer'. But next morning he woke up to find that some mischievous (or ingenious?) boys had scribbled below: 'But what is the question?' Through the centuries Christians have tried to discover the person, life and message of Jesus Christ through their own questions, emerging from their culture and society of the times. Should we deny the same to the Asia of today? Should one import answers into Asia, not caring for its questions? Let Asia then discover and rediscover the image of Jesus most suited to respond to the challenges of the continent and its questions. As a body of leaders in touch with the pastoral realities of Asia, FABC has made, and hopefully will continue to make, significant contributions to this task.

Notes

1. *For All the Peoples of Asia. Federation of Asian Bishops' Conferences. Documents from 1970 to 1991*, ed. Gaudencio B. Rosales and C. G. Arevalo, Quezon City and New York 1992. All the references to FABC documents, unless otherwise specified, are to this collection.

2. There is an entry under 'Jesus Christ', with just one reference, and that not to the Documents of FABC, but to the introductory essay.

3. So that there is no confusion, it should be stated here that whenever Asian bishops or Asia are mentioned, the reference is to those regions of Asia which come under the Federation of Asian Bishops' Conferences. The member conferences of the Federation are: Bangladesh, China, India-Nepal, Indonesia, Japan, Korea, Laos-Kampuchea, Malaysia-Singapore-Brunei, Myanmar (Burma), Pakistan, the Philippines, Sri Lanka, Thailand and Vietnam; the ecclesiastical jursidictions of Hong Kong and Macau enjoy associate membership. As can be seen, what from our geographical position we call West Asia (and referred to from the West as the Middle East) is not included in the Federation.

4. For a correct understanding of the various texts of FABC, it is important to hold the following facts in mind. The Federation generally convenes in Plenary Assembly

with the participation of presidents and delegates of member conferences once in four years, and it is the highest body. Up to now there have been five Plenary Assemblies: Taipei (1974); Calcutta (1978); Bangkok (1982); Tokyo (1986); Bandung (1990). But the different offices and institutes, etc., relating to various aspects of the life of the church, function regularly. Thus there are offices for mission, laity, social communication, human development, ecumenical and inter-religious affairs, education and students' chaplains. In addition there is also a Theological Advisory Committee which is at the service of FABC and its various organs.

5. To have an idea of the extent of poverty in Asia, it is enough to have a look at the recently published *Human Development Report 1992* of the United Nations Development Programme (UNDP), Oxford 1992. The report has depicted the world situation in the form of a champagne glass with a broad top and a progressively narrowing stem. Whereas the richest fifth of the world receives 82.7% of the total world income, the poorest fifth receives just 1.4% of the total world income. The overwhelming majority of Asian countries come under this latter group, with some exceptions like Japan. For the various issues and challenges in the continent, cf. Felix Wilfred, *Sunset in the East? Asian Challenges and Christian Involvement*, Madras 1991.

6. *Bishops Institute for Social Action* (BISA VII), organized by the Office for Human Development of FABC, 232.

7. The International Congress on Mission held in Manila (1979) with the participation of a large number of Asian bishops, the documents of which are incorporated in the FABC collection (n.1), stated: 'Unless the Church does her missionary activity with the firm conviction that the poor are ultimately the privileged community and agents of salvation (as has always been the case in the history of salvation), then that indispensable humility will be lacking, which alone reveals the truth about Christ, about man and about the Church herself' (144).

8. *Asian Bishops' Meeting*, Manila 1970, 5. This meeting, held on the occasion of the visit of Pope Paul VI, was the immediate inspiration for the founding of FABC.

9. Cf. *Statement of the FABC I Assembly*, 15.

10. The last Plenary Assembly held in Bandung, Indonesia, laid emphasis on the 'being' of the church. More than deeds, it called for a 'New way of being Church' in Asia, cf. 283, 287.

11. Cf. *Bishops Institute for Religious Affairs (BIRA) IV/12*, 331.

12. *Plenary Assembly V*, 279.

13. 'In order that we may discover our genuine and specific place in the multireligious cultural context of Asia, we need to rediscover Jesus Christ as the Liberator of Asia, and his Church as the servant and instrument of that liberation . . . Hence, the call today for us Asian Christians is to become a Church deeply committed to Jesus the Liberator' (*Statement of the Plenary Assembly IV*, 191).

14. Cf. for example, *Plenary Assembly I* (Taipei 1974), 13; *Plenary Assembly IV* (Tokyo 1986), 191.

15. The Kingdom of God is a Leitmotif in the documents, and its importance was re-affirmed forcibly by the last Plenary Assembly (Bandung 1990). For the statement cf. 273–89.

16. *Plenary Assembly I*, 14.

17. *Plenary Assembly IV* (Tokyo 1986), 182, 187.

18. Cf. *Ad Gentes* nos. 2 & 3.

19. Under the title *The Idea of the Church in the Documents of the Federation of Asian Bishops' Conferences (FABC) 1970–1982* the Indonesian theologian Carolus

Putranta submitted a doctoral thesis at the Gregorian University, Rome, 1985. The author gives a brief summary of his findings in the Collection of FABC documents (n. 1). On the role of the Spirit in the thought of the bishops, he states: 'In His Spirit, Christ continues to awaken and foster peoples' aspirations towards the fullness of life. As the Christian and the Church in Asia encounter the Spirit's activity, there must be an attitude of respectful listening and discerning: the role of the Christian in proclaiming the Name and Gospel of Christ is a "seconding" – a participation – in this presence and action of the Spirit in the world' (265).

20. Cf. *Nostra Aetate*, no. 1.

21. Cf. for example, *Plenary Assembly I* (Bandung 1990), 281ff.

22. Cf. *BIRA IV/6*, 304.

23. Being aware of the remarkable difference in the present historical context and the profound transformation taking place in Asia and in the Third World at large, the *International Mission Congress* held in Manila (1979) declared in its message: 'We have reached a decisive turning point in the mission history of the Third World. There is no return to the past, neither to the past mission theories, nor to past mission methods, nor to past mission goals' (131).

24. Cf. *BIRA IV/7*. 310; cf. also *Plenary Assembly V*, 282.

25. There is a rich distinctive missiological tradition in India and in Asia. This has been developed with the keen awareness that the local church is the bearer, the agent of mission in its context. As George Gispert-Sauch notes in reviewing the recent work of David J. Bosch (*Transforming Mission. Paradigm Shifts in Theology of Mission*, New York 1991), this rich tradition unfortunately tends to be neglected or taken little note of (*Vidyajyoti Journal of Theological Reflection* 56, 1992, 623–5).

26. *BIMA II*, 100; *BIRA II*, 115; *International Congress on Mission*, 129, 136–7.

27. The seriousness with which the bishops take the context came out when in the last Plenary Assembly they stated: 'This is the context of God's creative and redemptive action, the theatre in which the drama of Asia's salvation is enacted', *Plenary Assembly V* (Bandung 1990), 275.

28. Besides the collection of FABC documents (n. 1), cf. also *Theses on the Local Church. A Theological Reflection in the Asian Context*, a document by the Theological Advisory Commission of FABC (FABC Papers No. 60), Hong Kong 1991, especially thesis no. 10.

29. Cf. Alan Race, *Christians and Religious Pluralism. Patterns in the Christian Theology of Religions*, London 1983.

30. Cf. the various statements of BIRA. However, the further evolution of their thinking was already somewhat present in an important statement of the bishops on the relationship of the economy of salvation and various religious traditions. Out of their immediate and existential relationship with the religious universe of their neighbours, the bishops stated: 'In this dialogue we accept them (other religious traditions) as significant and positive elements in the economy of God's design of salvation. In them we recognize and respect profound spiritual and ethical meaning and values. Over many centuries they have been the treasury of the religious experience of our ancestors, from which our contemporaries do not cease to draw light and strength. They have been (and continue to be) the authentic expression of the noblest longings of their hearts, and the home of their contemplation and prayer. They have helped to give shape to the histories and cultures of our nations. How then can we not give them reverence and honour?' (14).

31. Cf. M. M. Thomas, *The Acknowledged Christ of the Indian Renaissance*,

London and Madras 1970; cf. also Felix Wilfred and M. M. Thomas, *Theologie-geschichte der Dritten Welt: Indien*, Munich 1992; Hans Staffner, *The Significance of Jesus Christ in Asia*, Anand 1985.

32. Cf. Christopher Duraisingh and Cecil Hargreaves (eds.), *India's Search for Reality and the Relevance of the Gospel of John*, Delhi 1975; George Soares-Prabhu (ed.), *Wir werden bei Ihm wohnen. Das Johannesevangelium in indischer Deutung*, Freiburg 1984.

Heart of the Matter

Re-Discovering the Core-Message of the New Testament in the Third World

Carlos H. Abesamis

This article is a 'report' on how we read or re-read the New Testament in the Third World, specifically in the Philippines. This re-reading lays claim to being a serious reading, making use of what is valid in the historico-critical method, and what is emerging as the sociological method. But its main exegetical instrument is solidarity with the struggling poor of the Third World and viewing things through the eyes of the poor, for this reading claims and demonstrates that the outlook of Jesus and the poor are kindred, if not identical. Thus to 'see things through the eyes of the poor' is to see things 'through the eyes of Jesus'. The language of this article will, for the most part, be simple – as the language of Jesus and the poor are simple. (One of the big sins of Christian theology is to use ten-letter words where five-letter words will do.)

Because of the length-limits of this article, this will have to be a partial report.

Jesus and salvation

Our study of the New Testament revolves around the question of 'Jesus and Salvation'. These two words summarize the core-message of the New Testament. It is important for the Christian consciousness to capture this core-message, for all the rest radiates from this centre and refers back to it. It is also quite vulnerable to misinterpretation. Thus it is worth the time and effort to get some clarity about it.

Since Jesus himself is the fountainhead of everything in the New Testament, we go back as much as possible to Jesus himself, his original message, sentiments and deeds. We do not at every turn prove the originality or authenticity of every word or deed of Jesus, but we feel there is authenticity when there is a criss-crossing attestation to it (for example, the proclamation of the Kingdom of God), when the same idea is disguised in different words (for example, the 'land' in Matt. 5.5, the 'new world' of Matt. 19.28 and the 'kingdom' of Luke 22.29–30), when something is such a commonplace in the culture of Jesus that it would be somewhat fantastic that Jesus would be ignorant of it (for example, the expectation of a new history, the 'age-to-come'), and when something fits in so well with the rest of Jesus' thought and life-context.

The mission of Jesus

In looking into this core-message, our first step is to ask the question: what was the mission of Jesus? We start with a dynamic question, not with abstract or metaphysical questions, such as those about the nature of Jesus or his messiahship.

The aim in this first step is to arrive at the following insight: although on the cross or from the vantage point of eternity Jesus' mission is spoken of by Sacred Scripture in terms of *Jesus' atoning death for sin*, still, on the plane of history and in an earlier phase in his life, Jesus' mission is presented by the same Sacred Scripture as having another focus, namely, the *Reign or Kingdom of God*. These two – Jesus' atoning death for sin and the coming of the Kingdom of God – though related (we will not now go into 'how') are *not* identical. The Kingdom of God did not materialize only at the death of Jesus. Already during his lifetime, Jesus categorically claimed that the Kingdom of God was 'in the midst of you' (Luke 17.21; cf. also Luke 11.20).

I do not know whether a theology inspired by the First World gives an adequate treatment to this question of the mission of Jesus. But it is critical. It can and does spell the difference between a pastoral activity and spirituality that concerns itself merely with bringing spiritual[1] salvation to people and another which concerns itself with enabling life in its fullest scope to flourish.

The common and normal answer

How do we go about arriving at a biblically and pastorally satisfying insight? We begin with the common and normal answer among average Christians, cleric or lay: Jesus' mission was to bring us salvation by dying for our sins. The principal theological or catechetical concepts associated with this answer are: *(a)* the *death* of Jesus as the salvific act of Jesus, *(b)* *expiation* and *forgiveness* of *sin*, *(c)* the *soul* as the target of salvation; a more updated theology would speak of the whole person,[2] *(d) spiritual grace* as the salvific blessing in this life, *(e) heaven* as the goal after death, *(f) face to face contemplation of God* as the form of final and definitive reward in the life after death, *(g) faith* on the part of the believer as the proper response.

It may surprise seminary professors to realize that this is still by and large the common understanding even among priests and pastors. I suspect that a partial reason for this state of affairs is that theological 'updatings' have not sufficiently tackled the significant questions connected with the mission of Jesus.

To set things in perspective, let us say at the outset that the power of the atoning death of Jesus is something one cannot underestimate. Such power and beauty have impacted, with varying degrees of intensity, on the hearts of martyrs, saints, fervent believers, and especially mystics who have tasted and smelled it in another dimension of 'knowing'. And on the day of true and universal ecumenism, the world will see that the atoning death of Jesus will be part of Christianity's contribution to the dialogue with Asian religions on sin, karma and self-realization.

However, to see Jesus' mission only in terms of his atoning death would be to impoverish the testimony of Sacred Scripture. What then do we say to this common and normal understanding? We say that it is correct and biblical, but incomplete. The New Testament, speaking from the vantage point of eternity, for example, does speak of Jesus' expiating death as his mission:

> In this is love, not that we loved God but that he loved us and sent his Son to be the expiation for our sins (I John 4.10; see also Rom. 5.6–10; John 3.16; Matt. 1.21; Mark 10.45; I Cor. 15.3ff.).

But we also say that it is incomplete!

Proclamation of the Reign or Kingdom of God

Why do we say that the traditional answer is incomplete? Because the biblical witness speaks of Jesus' mission *within history, before his death on the cross*, as focussed on the Reign or Kingdom of God[3] and its proclamation:

> Now after John was arrested, Jesus came into Galilee, preaching the gospel of God, and saying, 'The time is fulfilled, and the kingdom of God is at hand' (Mark 1.14–15; see also Matt. 4.17,23; 9.35; 24.24; Luke 4.43; 8.1; 9.11; Matt 3.2; 10.7; Luke 9.2; Luke 10.9–11 and Acts 1.3; 8.12; 19.8; 20.25; 28.23; 28.31).

About this text and similar ones, we note the following:

1. These are clearly mission-texts, that is to say, texts whose intention is to make a declaration about the mission of Jesus. (I have not included texts such as Matt 9.13; Mark 2.17; Luke 12.49; John 3.16–17; 9.39; 10.10, because in one sense or other they are 'secondary'.) This fact is evident from just a cursory reading. They state the mission of Jesus in summary form. If it is not that evident, try reading it out aloud with expression.

2. The spotlight of these mission-statements evidently falls on the Reign-Kingdom of God. It is clear that the mission of Jesus had somehow to do with the proclamation of what his culture called *malkuth shamayim* or the Reign-Kingdom of God. In fact, these texts and the whole gospel narrative declare that the one theme that threads together the Jesus-story was the proclamation of the Reign-Kingdom of God.

What is our concluding insight – given the fact that the Scripture speaks of both 1. the expiating death of Jesus and 2. his Reign-Kingdom-proclamation as his life-mission, and given the fact that these two are not identical? I think this is the way to do justice to the biblical evidence: *on the cross, the mission of Jesus was indeed to die for our sins, but initially, originally, in an earlier phase in his career, his mission was the proclamation of the Reign-Kingdom of God*. That is a simple and adequate enough way of stating the matter.

But one may also point out that biblical texts which deal with the mission of Jesus were written from different perspectives. From the perspective of *eternity*, there are numerous possible ways of speaking about the mission of Jesus, and some texts speak of that mission in terms of expiation of sin through his sacrificial death (so I John 4.10 above). But *inside history*, the mission of Jesus, *initially, that is, in an earlier phase in his life, was the proclamation of the Reign-Kingdom of God* (so Mark 1.14–15 above). So, when we contemplate things from eternity, we can say that Jesus' mission was to die for our sins. But when we insert ourselves *within history*, we should say that originally Jesus' mission was focussed on the Reign-Kingdom of God.

[At this early stage, we can draw attention to the fact that Jesus was indeed a proclaimer of salvation, but he proclaimed salvation not in terms of 'heaven' but in terms of the 'Reign-Kingdom of God'! Heaven and Reign-Kingdom of God are not identical, as we shall eventually see. This can be a shocking revelation, but this little bit of information could help us pastorally to think and talk more in terms of Reign-Kingdom rather than just heaven – and to accept the implications and consequences of such Reign-Kingdom language.]

Reign-Kingdom of God as reconstructed from the Beatitudes

This brings us to the question: and what is the Reign-Kingdom of God? Here we let the biblical witness speak again. But by way of introduction, let me mention some common misconceptions. The first is that the Kingdom of God is identical with heaven. In keeping with this, Jesus is inviting us to heaven, Jesus is opening the gates of heaven and so forth. But there is no such thing in the Bible. The second is that the Kingdom of God is identical with the church. Again, there is no such thing in the mind of Jesus. The third is that Reign of God means God's reign in our hearts, where the Kingdom of God is reduced to a purely interior reality in the heart. This involves a mis-reading of Luke 17.20–21, where the text is inaccurately rendered as 'The Reign-Kingdom of God is within you', whereas it should be read correctly, in the context of Jesus' ministry: 'The Reign-Kingdom of God is *among* you.'

What then is the Reign-Kingdom of God – biblically speaking, or more accurately, as Jesus conceived it? In essence, it is a new world experiencing a new history. The Jews in Jesus' time conceived it as a new Israel and a new history for Israel. It involves a new earth where instead of poverty and oppression there is justice and liberation; where instead of hunger there is bread and rice; instead of sorrow, there is laughter; where the land belongs to the meek; where the compassionate will be repaid with compassion; where we have the direct experience of God; where we finally attain to the full status of the sons and daughters of God. In keeping with this biblical spirit, an Asian, anticipating the Reign-Kingdom of God, would be looking forward to a new Asia, experiencing a new Asian history, where one experiences the definitive blessings of life – health, food, God's presence – in all its fullness.

The Kingdom of God based on the Beatitudes

How do we come to such an interpretation of the Reign-Kingdom of God? By understanding the Beatitudes as Jesus understood them. Look up Matt. 5.3–10; Luke 6.20–21.

There are some guidelines for understanding the Beatitudes with a view to discovering the meaning of Reign-Kingdom of God:

1. The Beatitudes are proclamations of salvation. Jesus was announcing salvation to various groups, such as the hungry, the pure in heart, the meek, etc. Read the Beatitudes aloud properly. They should sound like ringing announcements of salvation:

Blessed are the pure in heart, for they shall see God!
Blessed are the meek, for they shall inherit the earth!

To the pure in heart he was proclaiming salvation in the form of the vision of God. To the meek, he was proclaiming salvation in the form of possession of the land.

2. Salvation and Reign-Kingdom of God were identical. When the Jews thought or talked about salvation, they thought and talked in terms of the Reign-Kingdom of God.

3. And where in the Beatitudes should we look? The second part. Each Beatitude has two parts. For example:

> Blessed are the meek, for they shall inherit the land.
>   (first part)   (second part)

It is the second part that contains the various blessings of salvation or of the Reign-Kingdom of God. Thus the second part is a term or a name for salvation. It contains an aspect or description of the Reign-Kingdom of God.

With such guidelines, we see that salvation or the Reign-Kingdom of God means:

. . . they shall be called sons of God (Matt.)

To attain to the (full) status of sons and daughters of God.

. . . they shall see God (Matt.)

To see and experience God directly. At present, we see God darkly, as in a metal mirror. Salvation or Reign-Kingdom of God will entail the direct experience of God.

. . . they shall obtain mercy (Matt.)

To obtain compassion. Compassion here is the Old Testament *hesed*, which in the prophetic oracles 'is the compassion that is intimately associated with justice (*mishpat* or *sedakah*) and faithfulness (*'emet*) to form what today we would call social justice'.[4] Thus to obtain compassion means to experience social justice with the peculiar flavour of compassion.

. . . they shall inherit the earth (Matt.)

Land! Earth! This is not a spiritualized earth. It is the earth that you touch and smell. It is the same earth/land of Deuteronomy and Psalms.[5] The millions of landless peasants in the Third World long and struggle for this kind of land.

... you shall laugh (Luke) ... they shall be comforted (Matt.)

Comfort and laughter for those who 'mourn' and 'weep'. These mourning and weeping people, like the 'poor' and the 'hungry' in the other Beatitudes, refer to the oppressed poor in Palestinian society in Jesus' time. So here, the Kingdom of God consists in comfort and joy for the poor and oppressed.

... you shall be satisfied (Luke)

Satisfaction of hunger, or, in other words, *food, bread, oil, fruit of the vine*. This food is not metaphorical nor purely symbolic. This is shown in a petition in the Lord's prayer, 'Give us this day our "daily" bread'. 'Daily' is not the only possible translation of the original Greek *epiousion*. It can also be translated 'for tomorrow', in which case it applies to the bread of the Kingdom of God which was expected to come 'tomorrow' or in the future. In the prayer as Jesus originally taught it, Jesus was referring not to the day-to-day bread, but to the bread of the Kingdom which they were expecting to come in the future. Now, we ourselves are witnesses to the fact that when, in the Lord's Prayer, we pray God to give us bread, we certainly are not praying for metaphorical or symbolic bread, nor for spiritual bread (only). We pray for real bread! In other words, the tone of the Lord's Prayer is such that real, not merely symbolic, bread, is meant. Couple this with the fact that the bread of the Lord's prayer originally referred to the bread of the Kingdom and we see that we cannot limit Reign-Kingdom food to something symbolic only.[6]

Blessed are you poor, for yours is the kingdom of God (Luke)

Finally, the Reign-Kingdom of God means *justice and liberation of the poor and oppressed*. To come to this insight, one takes into account that: 1. the

Blessed are the poor in spirit, for theirs is the kingdom of heaven (Matt.)

'*anawin* of the original Beatitude referred not only to the poor but to the poor *and oppressed*.[7] 2. The Beatitude, like other Beatitudes, is a proclamation of salvation. If we put these two guidelines together – that is, if we ask what is the salvation to be proclaimed to the poor and oppressed – we see that implied in the 'Kingdom of God'[8] in this Beatitude is justice and liberation of the poor and oppressed.

Other cautions

We have said enough to get an idea of how we get at the Kingdom of God through the Beatitudes. But for a more secure grasp, we take time to note the following:

1. In reconstructing the Kingdom of God, focus the search on the second part of the Beatitude, for it is there that you will find the answer to the question: what is the Kingdom of God? Do *not* look at the *first* part, for it contains, not what the Kingdom of God is, but *who* will receive the Kingdom of God. It does not contain the blessings that make up the Kingdom of God, but the recipients, the candidates. Otherwise you would have to make such absurd statements as: the Kingdom of God is the poor, the hungry . . .

2. Beware also of reading the Beatitudes as imperatives or counsels to virtue. When Jesus said, 'Blessed are the hungry . . . ', he did not mean, 'Be hungry. It is good to be hungry. Hunger is a Christian virtue. It is your ticket to heaven.' No, the Beatitudes were not meant to be moral imperatives or exhortations to virtue or conditions for entering heaven. They are rather proclamations of salvation. 'To you who are hungry, I proclaim satisfaction of hunger!' To use big words, the Beatitudes are not *paraenesis* (exhortation), they are *kerygma* (announcement, proclamation).

The resultant portrait of the Kingdom of God in the Beatitudes

The Reign-Kingdom of God, based on the Beatitudes, is a new world and a new history, where the poor have been delivered from poverty, where those who mourned now rejoice, where there is no hunger, where the land now belongs to the humble(d), where people who have shown compassion will experience compassion, where people have a direct experience of God and his fatherhood.

Reign-Kingdom of God as reconstructed from Jesus' words based on Isaiah

We fill out a little more our understanding of Reign-Kingdom of God. Another main source for reconstructing its meaning are words of Jesus, based on Isaiah. The point to grasp in this exercise is that the Reign-Kingdom is to be found where life-blessings such as these are present:

> health to the sick,
> life or resurrection for the dead,
> good news of deliverance from poverty,
> liberty to captives,
> proclamation of the final jubilee year (cf. Lev. 25),
> joy for the poor,
> someone anointed by the Spirit of God,
> a chosen servant who
> > will bring good tidings to the poor, etc.,
> > will bring forth justice to the nations.

This is the portrait of Reign-Kingdom which emerges from certain words of Jesus, a portrait which is inspired by the texts from Isaiah.

Isaiah and Jesus

How do we arrive at this insight? First, by recognizing in the writings of Isaiah a picture of salvation with its many features and recognizing the Reign of God as one of such features. Second, by realizing that Reign of God is, in a practical way of speaking, really the sum-total of all the other features with which it is associated. In other words, God's reign is present when the features or blessings with which it is associated are present. Third, by seeing Jesus' words as echoing the images, vocabulary and spirit of Isaiah. Concretely, then:

1. In Isaiah we find a picture of salvation. We note that the book(s) of Isaiah as they existed in the time of Jesus formed one organic unit: not divided into chapters and verse.[9] Thus in reading Isaiah in the time of Jesus, one would get one organic picture of salvation. For lack of space, instead of quoting all the texts, I will lift the key-words that depict salvation from some sample texts:

> Good news
> Your God reigns! (Isa. 52.7).

> Good news
> Here is your God! (or: The reign of God is manifest) (Isa. 40.9).

The eyes of the blind shall be opened
and the ears of the deaf unstopped
(Isa. 35.5–6).

The *'anāwim* (poor and oppressed) will ever find joy in
the Lord
and the poor rejoice in the Holy One of Israel
(Isa. 29.18–19).

The Spirit of the Lord God is upon me,
because the Lord has anointed me
to bring good news to the poor (*'anāwim*).
he has sent me to bind up the brokenhearted,
to proclaim liberty to the captives,
and the opening of the prison to those who are
bound;
to proclaim the year of the Lord's favour
(Isa. 61.1–2).

. . . to let the oppressed go free (Isa. 58.6).

Here is my servant whom I uphold,
my chosen one with whom I am pleased.
Upon whom I have put my Spirit;
he shall bring forth justice to the nations.
Not crying out, not shouting, not making his voice heard
in the street.
A bruised reed he shall not break,
and a smouldering wick he shall not quench.
Until he establishes justice on the earth,
the coastlands will wait for his teaching
(Isa. 42.1–4).

Thy dead will live, their bodies shall rise
(Isa. 25.8).

2. And what is God's reign practically speaking? It is nothing else than
all the other features or life-blessings with which it is associated. Thus the
Reign-Kingdom consists in:

Sight to the blind
health to the lame
hearing to the deaf
life to the dead

the good news of deliverance to the poor
freedom for captives
liberation to the oppressed
the final jubilee year (cf. Lev. 25).

3. Jesus then echoes the ideas, images, words of Isaiah. Note that these words of Jesus were spoken in separate incidents in his life, and often contain only partial allusions to Isaiah. In reading the Jesus texts, we have to be alert to what is implied or alluded to. The highlighted words reflect Jesus' understanding of Kingdom of God:

> Go and tell John what you hear and see:
> *the blind receive their sight*
> *and the lame walk*,
> lepers are cleansed
> *and the deaf hear*,
> *and the dead are raised up*,
> *and the poor have good news preached to them*.
> And blessed is he who takes no offence at me
> (Matt. 11.2–6).

(Note, then, that although the term 'Reign-Kingdom' is not mentioned by Jesus here, the allusion to it is clear, and the life-blessings enumerated are the Isaianic blessings of the Reign of God.)

> Now after John was arrested, Jesus came into Galilee, proclaiming the *good news* of God, and saying, 'The time is fulfilled, and the *Kingdom of God* is at hand; repent, and believe the good news'
> (Mark 1.14–15).

(This text, on the other hand, mentions the term 'Kingdom of God' but does not enumerate the blessings of the Kingdom. But since 'good news' coupled with 'Kingdom' has an Isaianic ring, the Isaianic blessings are implied here.)

Here are other words of or about Jesus in which Reign-Kingdom and salvation are expressed or implied:

> And he came to Nazareth, where he had been brought up;
> and he went to the synagogue, as his custom was, on the
> sabbath day.
> And he stood up to read; and there was given to him the
> book of the prophet Isaiah. He opened the book and found
> the place where it was written,
> *'The Spirit of the Lord is upon me,*

because he has anointed me
to preach good news to the poor.
He has sent me *to proclaim release to the captives*
and *recovering of sight to the blind,*
to set at liberty those who are oppressed,
to proclaim the acceptable year of the Lord.
And he closed the book, and gave it back to the
attendant, and sat down; and the eyes of all in the
synagogue were fixed on him. And he began to say to them,
'Today this scripture has been fulfilled in your hearing'
(Luke 4.16–21).
This was to fulfil what was spoken by the prophet
Isaiah:
'Behold, *my servant whom I have chosen, my beloved with*
whom my soul is well pleased.
I will put my Spirit upon him,
and he shall proclaim justice to the nations.
He will not wrangle or cry aloud, nor will any one hear
his voice in the streets;
he will not break a bruised reed or quench a smouldering
wick,
till he brings justice to victory;
and in his name will the nations hope'
(Matt. 12.17–21).

Even the following text, the Beatitude on the poor, is inspired by Isaiah,
where the happiness of the poor is associated with the Reign of God.

'Blessed are you poor, for yours is the Reign-Kingdom of God'
(Luke 6.20).

A footnote on heaven and Kingdom
   Now that we have reconstructed the biblical meaning of Reign-
Kingdom of God, we see that biblically speaking, 'heaven' is not the same
as 'Kingdom of God'. For the Bible, there is indeed a place called 'heaven'
(Mark 1.9–11; Matt. 18.10; Eph. 1.9–10). But heaven is not the same
thing as Kingdom of God. The principal meaning of heaven is 'the
dwelling place of God up there' (Matt. 5.16; 7.11; 18.10; 6.9). It is also
where God's messengers, the angels, are (Matt. 22.30; 24.36). It also
coincides with the place where the righteous go after the moment of death.
But it is not spoken of as a new world or transformed creation (Matt. 19.28)
where there is food for the hungry (Luke 6.21), resurrection of the dead

(John 11.25; Matt. 11.5), unity of Christ with all created things in the universe (Eph. 1.10, etc.), which is what the Kingdom of God is.

To end

Our efforts thus far yield the simple, but for us in the Third World, consequential, reading: the mission of Jesus before he died on the cross was focussed on the Reign-Kingdom of God, which is a new world and a new history . . .

Our reading goes on to discover:

. . . that the resurrection is another feature of the Reign-Kingdom of God; that the biblical concern is for the total person.

. . . that another feature of the Reign-Kingdom of God is the destruction of evil powers.

. . . that the Reign-Kingdom of God is a *new world* or a *new creation*; that one picturesque phrase for new world in the New Testament is 'new heaven and new earth'.

. . . that another name for Reign-Kingdom of God is the 'age-to-come', which refers to a *new and alternative history*.

. . . that the Reign-Kingdom of God has a future aspect; that this future is not the moment of death of each individual but the end of this presently ongoing history, when the new world and new history, which we call the Reign-Kingdom of God, will come about; that there is indeed a life-after-death or 'going to heaven' when each individual dies, but that this is not identical with the Reign-Kingdom of God.

. . . that the Reign-Kingdom of God also has a present aspect; that in the time of Jesus the Reign-Kingdom of God was to be 'localized' in such life-blessings as those that Jesus wrought through his actions – health to the sick, life to the dead, good news of liberation to the poor; that in our time the Reign-Kingdom of God should be present in life-blessings proper to the needs of our time.

. . . that the Reign-Kingdom of God is both a goal and a task; that, as the terminal reward to which we are invited to enter in the future, it is a goal; that, because Jesus sent out his followers on a mission to proclaim the Kingdom in word and action, the Reign-Kingdom of God is also a task.

. . . that contemplative silence, such as the contemplation that Jesus practised, is an integral part of a Kingdom-oriented spirituality.

. . . that the good news of justice and liberation of the poor is a central concern of Jesus.

. . . that there is a 'gospel' aspect and a 'law' aspect in the New Testament.

. . . that the Kingdom-practice of Jesus was a conflictive practice; that in this conflict Jesus was clearly on the side of the poor and marginalized.

. . . that in reflecting on Jesus' death, one must take into account not only the faith-significance of his death (Why did Jesus die? He died in atonement for the sins of humankind) but also the historical causes ('Why was Jesus killed?').

. . . that the resurrection of Jesus was seen as the beginning of the new world; and the risen Jesus, as the indwelling Spirit and as the first fruits of that new world.

. . . that the expected parousia of Jesus was seen as a moment of joy and a moment of salvation because that is also the moment of the coming of the definitive Reign-Kingdom of God.

. . . that in a discourse on 'Jesus and Salvation', the over-arching reality in Jesus' career is the Reign-Kingdom of God and not narrowly the so-called 'paschal mystery'; and that the salvific action of Jesus is not to be confined to his death (and resurrection), but rather encompasses his ministry-death-resurrection-parousia.

Notes

1. I am using 'spiritual' here in the Greek sense, in which, after making the division into 'body' and 'soul', it calls 'spiritual' those things which pertain to the soul. This is different from the Hebrew sense, in which 'spiritual' refers, not to the soul, but to the total person or whatever reality is endowed with the Spirit of God.

2. This focus on the whole person, rather than merely soul, does not, however, significantly alter the basic thrust of this common and normal outlook. It remains basically moralistic and ahistorical.

3. The Hebrew word *malkuth* can mean either 'Reign' or 'Kingdom' or both. In this article, I use 'Reign' or 'Kingdom' or 'Reign-Kingdom' interchangeably.

4. For example, Hos 2.19–20; Micah 6.8; Isa. 32.15–16; Jer. 9.24.

5. For example, Deut. 1.8 and *passim*; Ps. 25.13; 37.9,11,22,29,34.

6. We tackled Luke's version which speaks about hunger for and satisfaction with material food, because the Lukan version has more chances of being closer to what Jesus actually said, whereas Matthew's version, which speaks of hunger and thirst for righteousness, shows up Matthew's special interest in the theme of righteousness.

7. The demonstration for this and for the choice of Matthew ('poor in spirit') rather than Luke would be too long to include in this article.

8. Kingdom of *heaven* is exactly the same as kingdom of *God*, the word 'heaven' functioning here as a substitute for the word 'God'. The Jews, out of respect for the name of God, substituted other words such as 'heaven'. Therefore, 'kingdom of heaven' does not refer to 'heaven'.

9. Much less into two or three books, as modern scholarship does.

Christian Incarnation and Hindu Avatara

Francis X. D'Sa

But though Christ and Krishna are the same, they are the same in difference, that is indeed the utility of so many manifestations instead of there being only one as these missionaries would have it. But is it really because the historical Christ has been made too much the foundation-stone of the Faith that Christianity is failing? (*Sri Aurobindo*)[1]

Introduction

The notorious dilemma between truth and method is unavoidable in any study of a religion or religious belief. On the one hand method cannot by itself lead to the 'truth' of a religious belief and on the other the lack of method fails in the long run to meet the challenge of superstition and fundamentalism.

Methodological remarks

The difficulty becomes almost insurmountable when it is a question of studying beliefs which are at home in a world-view different from one's own. Unfortunately the phrase 'Incarnation in Asian Thought' (the topic assigned to me) may *sound* innocuous to Western readers who have grown up in a Christian way of thinking and believing. The repeated use of terms like 'incarnation' in the context of Asian religions tends to make one overlook the fact that such phrases imperialistically carry over their specific flavour (derived from the soil of Western culture) to a vastly different metaphor-world where the distinctive taste of its own metaphors like avatara is subdued, if not suppressed. Thus 'Incarnation in Asian Thought' would be as innocuous as 'Avataras in European Thought' to Asian readers.

The way out of this impasse would be one that leads to the awareness of a specific metaphor-world and at the same time respects the primary claim of truth. Whatever the chances of success, the enterprise demands that we reflect critically on the procedures we adopt to enter the world of religion and the methods we employ in studying them.

With regard to our theme it is necesary to become thematically aware of the fact that an avatara is at home in a cosmocentric and incarnation in an anthropocentric world-view.[2] To one who has grown up in one world [-view] only and has had little or no contact with another this will not make much sense. Only the one who is aware of the differences in the two world-views will be on the search for an interface that can link the one with the other because he is in touch with both of them existentially, not merely cerebrally. Obviously such methodological awareness cannot itself be reduced to any method; however, it can be made operative through thematization, not unlike a system-file in a computer which though operative cannot be opened.

The language of symbol and metaphor

There is a further point that needs explicitation before proceeding to our reflection on avataras, and that is the symbolic nature of religious language. The language of belief, any belief, is symbolic. We can speak of [belief in the] avataras only within the world of symbol and metaphor. Because belief is an expression of a depth-experience it is to be distinguished from doctrine which (though popularly understood as belief) is in fact the attempt [of a later age] to reinterpret the belief in the language of the reinterpreting community. Belief, then, as an expression of a depth-experience, belongs to a primordial activity and as such is irreducible to either knowing or willing. A primordial activity has its own specific dynamism. That of belief which expresses itself in metaphor and parable tends primarily towards an extension, not of our information but of the 'frontiers of our being'. The result is that the believer perceives the world differently. With that, what formerly did not make sense to him (like self-giving or forgiving) begins to do so now.

The divine: the depth-dimension of reality

Religion is the quest for meaning in all its dimensions. Trying to see the wholeness of reality is another way of putting it, and a third approach might stress work for the welfare of all beings. However one might express it, religion has to do with the search for ultimate meaning thanks to which meaning becomes meaningful. If meaning is the body of a belief, meaningfulness would constitute its 'soul'. In one way or another everyone is in search of meaningfulness. The ultimacy of meaning has to do with the depth-dimension of reality and can express itself in a variety of ways. For belief being the outcome of the discovery of the depth-dimension of reality, meaningfulness is the manifestation of this discovery and is encountered in its human as well as in its cosmic aspects. Hence to speak of the depth-dimension as the divine is only one of many possible approaches.

Avatara and vibhuti

The Hindu tradition has articulated its experience of the depth-dimension in a variety of ways.[3] Of these the two most important are avatara and vibhuti: the former stresses the aspect of presence and the latter that of power. We have avatara when the divine descends into this world and becomes present in one form (= nature) or another. But in the case of the vibhuti the divine is not [fully] present, since a vibhuti represents only an aspect of the divine and is encountered when the divine equips someone or something with the gift of its power. Whereas in the avatara it is the divine itself which takes on the nature (i.e. the form) of, say, a fish or a boar or a human being, in the vibhuti a special divine power or quality is at work.

The avataras

Though belief in the avataras is not explicit in the canonical scriptures, it is part and parcel of the Hindu tradition. The reason is that it is the *vox populi* that proclaims in the course of its history the descent of the avatara into this world. Hence it is not surprising that the Hindu traditions have produced a variety of avatara schemes. Of all these, the one of the ten avataras[4] has become classical. This is how the modern mystic-philosopher Aurobindo Ghosh views it:

> The Hindu procession of the ten Avatars is itself, as it were, a parable of evolution. First the Fish Avatar, then the amphibious animal between land and water, then the land animal, then the Man-Lion Avatar, bridging man and animal, then man as dwarf, small and undeveloped and physical but containing in himself the godhead and taking possession of existence, then the rajasic, sattwic, nirguna Avatars, leading the human development from the vital rajasic to the sattwic mental man and again the overmental superman. Krishna, Buddha and Kalki depict the last three stages, the stages of the spiritual development – Krishna opens the possibility of overmind, Buddha tries to shoot

beyond to the supreme liberation but that liberation is still negative, not returning upon earth to complete positively the evolution; Kalki is to correct this by bringing the Kingdom of the Divine upon earth, destroying the opposing Asura forces. The progression is striking and unmistakable.[5]

The avatara doctrine

An avatara scheme like this is significant only within the world of the avatara belief. The entry to this world could be the divine poem *Bhagavadgita*, Chapter 4 of which (vv.6–9) contains the *locus classicus* :

> Unborn, imperishable in my own being, and Lord over finite lives,
> Still I take as my basis material existence and appear through my own power.
> For whenever right languishes
> And unright ascends, I manifest myself.
> Age after age I appear to establish the right and true,
> So that the good are saved and the evildoers perish.
> When a man knows my divine birth and work thus, as they really are,
> After this life he is not reborn, but comes to me.
> Many people, freed of passion, fear, and anger, full of me and relying on me,
> Have been purified by the fire of wisdom and have come to my mansion.[6]

Any interpretation of the 'becoming' of the divine into the world of space and time has to take into account the following points. The avatara passage begins with unambiguous and insistent assertions – much more striking in the Sanskrit original than in the translation – of the unchangeable nature of the divine. Secondly, the supremacy of the divine is clearly proclaimed. Thirdly, the unchangeable divine enters the realm of change (= the cosmic). Fourthly, he does so on his own. Fifthly, the *occasion* for his manifestation is announced: the decline of dharma and the rise of its opposite. Sixthly, the *purpose* and occasion of the divine manifestation which occurs in every age is the protection of the good, the destruction of evildoers and the restoration of dharma. Finally, the *aim* of the avatara belief is to liberate the believer from rebirth.

The avatara belief: seeing all things in the divine

The belief is to be understood in a manner that does justice to the above considerations, though obviously it can be reduced to them. The passage asserts the birth of the divine within the context of divine immutability and promises to lead to liberation the one acquainted with this mystery. To know the divine birth and work means freedom from rebirth and entrance into the divine. A connection is thus made between his perduring presence and the liberating knowledge of his birth and action. These are in consonance with divine immutability.

If the occasion for the 'becoming' of the avatara is the increase of evil and the decline of goodness in this world, then this is true of every age. For of which age could it not be said that evil has taken the upper hand? Is it not the general belief, especially among 'good' people, that the 'present' age is characterized by a progressive decline in the practice of morality? Is it not our tendency to consider the age we live in as 'evil', and to look back nostalgically at the past (especially the hoary past) as the 'golden age'? This is true of every age. Hence the statement (4.8) that the divine becomes into this world 'age after age' (i.e. in every age). Every age then is the occasion for the Absolute to 'take birth' in order to 'work' for the restoration of dharma. The question is how in the context of the repeated assertions about the immutability of the divine we are to understand his coming.

In the cosmocentric world-view 'he really becomes' cannot mean a historical coming – because he is always present! His coming can only mean our becoming aware of the effects of his presence and his power – especially when everything looks dark and dismal.

This point needs some elaboration, since the danger of interpreting it merely psychologically is real. Knowing is not what goes on inside the head of the knower; knowing is becoming what we already are. We are part of, not apart from, reality. Through knowing we realize this oneness or, better still, we let this oneness become operative in our lives, albeit only step by step. Against this background, 'becoming aware' means realizing our oneness with reality.

The Hindu experience of the human does not imply historicity in the way in which Christian-Western experience of the last centuries does because the Hindu understanding of the experience of 'being-in-the-world' is such that prakriti (i.e. the mutable), not purusha (the immutable), is part and parcel of the world. The Hindu's utter lack of interest in any kind of quest for the historical Krishna suggests how Krishna is believed to be present in the world of space and time: he is and operates *in* the world but he is not *of* the world. Moreover in the cosmocentric tradition the divine is conceived in terms of the cosmic rather than the personal. Thus we can say that Krishna *is*; but we cannot say that he is *there* because his presence is co-terminous with all that is.

In contrast to the Western historical world-view where presence connotes historicity, on the Hindu side it is ontological. In the former, ontology is grounded in a historical horizon of understanding; in the latter history is grounded in an ontological horizon of understanding.

The avatara belief highlights the dynamic manner in which divine presence operates in this world; the primary purpose of the belief is not meant to promote adoration and worship but to provide inspiration and courage in moments of hopelessness when evil replacing goodness acts supreme, and to remind the believer that the divine mystery remains always in control of this world and that nothing happens without his knowledge and consent. This belief leaves no room for despair or fatalism.

The avatara conception implies that the divine is fully the agent and that behind that agent there is no other personality to whom agency could be attributed. An avatara is the divine in the form into which it has descended. The Krishna avatara, for example, is the divine in the form of the human. Analogous to the distinction in the West between person and nature, in the Hindu traditions there is the distinction between individual (jˆva) and person (purusha).[7] This would permit us to state that the Krishna-avatara is both divine and a fully free human being, though not an individual in bondage.[8] This is because in traditional Hindu understanding every individual is caught up in the net of rebirth – a thing that cannot be said of Krishna. He is indeed human, but he transcends the cycle of birth and rebirth. Here being human does not necessarily imply historicity; historicity is peculiar only to those who are subject to bondage.

Hence *the avatara belief is basically an expression of the fundamental experience of the pervasive presence of the divine*: in this presence both the human and the cosmic are grounded. This explains both the multiplicity and the epochally recurrent pattern of the avataras. To expect anything else in the cosmocentric world-view would be to extrapolate from the anthropocentric world-view characteristics like uniqueness (of the *eph'hapax* type).

The avatara belief conveys in a dramatic way the fact that the divine is a constitutive dimension of reality. Evil is the absence of the divine. But the experience of the absence of the divine is not at all a bad preparation for the arrival of the divine.

Vibhutis: the divine manifestations

There is another way in which the divine is experienced in the Hindu traditions and that is known as vibhuti. A vibhuti is the manifestation of the divine at work in a person ('I am Arjuna among the Pandava Princes') or thing through a quality ('I am the taste in water') or even a happening ('I am death the destroyer of all'). The variety of divine manifestations that is part and parcel of a cosmocentric world-view encompasses practically everything. Though the popular axiom 'among beings the best or the first of its kind is a vibhuti' is not accurate enough, still it has a point. Whatever is exemplary, outstanding, unique, brilliant, marvellous, conspicuous, remarkable, striking, prominent or significant – all this is a vibhuti and is spoken of in different ways in the *Bhagavadgita*: 'All that exists is woven on me like a web of pearls on thread' (7.7); 'I am the source of everything, and everything proceeds from me' (10.7); 'I am the seed of all creatures' (10.39) and 'I stand sustaining this entire universe with a fragment of my being' (10.41).

The vibhuti doctrine

The following examples from the *Gita* could exemplify the doctrine of the vibhutis.

I am the taste in water . . . the light in the moon and sun, OM resonant in all sacred lore, the sound in space, valour in men. I am the pure fragrance in earth, the brilliance in fire, the life in all living creatures, the penance in ascetics, of strong men I am strength, without the emotion of desire; in creatures I am the desire that does not impede sacred duty (*Bhagavadgita* 7.8,9,11).

I am the self abiding in the heart of all creatures; I am their beginning, their middle and their end. I am Vishnu striding among sun gods, the radiant sun among lights; I am lightning among wind gods, the moon among the stars. I am the song in sacred lore; I am Indra, king of the gods; I am the mind of the senses, the consciousness of creatures . . . I am golden Meru towering over the mountains . . . I am the ocean of lakes . . . I am Himalaya, the measure of what endures . . . Among trees, I am the sacred fig-tree. I am chief of the divine sages, leader of the celestial musicians, the recluse philosopher among saints . . . among elephants, the divine king's mount; among men, the king . . . I am the procreative god of love, the king of the snakes . . . of measures, I am time; I am the lion among wild animals. I am the purifying wind . . . the flowing river Ganges. I am the beginning, the middle and the end of creations . . . of sciences, I am the science of the self . . . I am the vowel *a* of the syllabary . . . I am indestructible time, the creator facing everywhere at once. I am death the destroyer of all, the source of what will be, the feminine powers: fame, fortune, speech, memory, intelligence, resolve, patience . . . I am the great ritual chant, the metre of sacred song, the most sacred month in the year, the spring blooming with flowers . . . I am Krishna among my mighty kinsmen; I am Arjuna among the Pandava princes . . . I am the sceptre of rulers . . . I am the silence of mysteries, what men of knowledge know . . . I am the seed of all creatures; nothing animate or inanimate could exist without me (*Bhagavadgita* 10.20–39).[9]

These examples give us an inkling of some of the things and persons which are believed to be vibhutis. Taken from the cosmic elements and functions, from inanimate and animate things of the world, from human beings and their behaviour, they represent all that humankind holds to be sacred, significant and secure.

The vibhuti belief: seeing the divine in all things

The question is: 'What does all this mean? What is meant by manifestation of divine presence?' If in the avatara belief the divine presence and its supremacy over all beings is stressed with a view to fighting in times of trial and tribulation against hopelessness and despair, the vibhuti belief is a belief for 'all seasons'. *Everywhere and in everything the working of the Divine Presence is to be discerned*: not only in the good and the great, the brave and the beautiful, the proud and the powerful, but also in the obvious (like the wind and the water) and the dubious (like dice and desire). Nothing is left out, not even death 'the destroyer of all' (10.34).

Going the various kinds of vibhutis, one might be tempted to conclude that the divine has made an 'option for the best and the brave, the fair and the famous'. This would be a grave misreading. What the vibhuti belief intends to make clear is the opposite: whatever your achievements, your strengths, your talents and your origin, 'I dwell deep in the heart of everyone; memory, knowledge, and reasoning come from me; I am the object to be known through all sacred lore; and I am its knower, the creator of its final truth' (15.15).

A vibhuti is not a mere reminder that the divine mystery is at work in flesh, flower and fruit. It is an invitation to an encounter with the divine presence in and through the sacramentality of the cosmic dimension of reality. A vibhuti is, to use a hallowed Christian expression, a sacrament, and like every sacrament it invites us to cultivate a sacra-*mentality vis à vis* this universe.

Conclusion

Belief in the presence of the divine mystery, whether in the form of avatara or vibhuti, is a remarkable one. Remarkable not only because of its widespread hold on the people of the sub-continent (in spite of the fact that neither of them is part of the Hindu scriptural canon), but more because of its potential for social change. The actualization of this belief would mean the discovery of the depth-dimension both of the human and the cosmic; that is to say, it would initiate the dawn of a new world of relationships where humankind will have a different attitude, a be-attitude (and not a have-attitude) towards the universe; then the universe, in her turn, will reveal the source and substance of her richness.

Notes

N.B. *For typographical reasons I have unified the transliteration of Sanskrit words even in the case of titles and quotations.*

1. 'The Purpose of Avatarhood', *Letters on Yoga*, Sri Aurobindo Birth Centenary Library 22, Pondicherry 1970, 430.

2. Cf. F. X. D'Sa, *Gott, der Dreieine und der All-Ganze. Vorwort zur Begegnung zwischen Christentum und Hinduismus*, Theologie Interkulturell, Düsseldorf 1987, 5–78.

3. Cf. P. Hacker, 'Zur Entwicklung der Avataralehre', *Wiener Zeitschrift für die Kunde Südost-Asiens* 4, 1960, 47–60.

4. From among the different schemes, the ten-avatara scheme is the one which has won wide acceptance. We have other avatara schemes where the number of avataras ranges from six to twenty-three (cf. M. Dhavamony, 'Hindu Incarnations', *Studia Missionalia* 20, 1971, 163–89).

5. Aurobindo, 'Avatarhood' (n. 1), 402.

6. The translation is from Kees W. Bolle, *The Bhagavadgita. A New Translation*, Berkeley, Los Angeles and London 1979.

7. For the sake of clarity one must add that there is a difference in background for the distinction in the two instances: whereas in the Western tradition its background is philosophical, in the Hindu tradition it is soteriological.

8. The classical Hindu texts insist that Krishna was *like* a human; the reason is not to deny that he was a real human being but to highlight the fact that he stands in a class by himself; on this backdrop, to be human applies to be in bondage. Here historicity implies bondage. But this is not true of Krishna, because he is never in bondage. Misunderstanding this, some non-Hindus conclude that the doctrine of the avatara is a sort of docetism. Cf. J. Neuner, 'Das Christus-Mysterium und die indische Lehre von den Avataras', *Das Konzil von Chalkedon. Geschichte und Gegenwart III*, ed. A. Grillmeier and H. Bacht, Würzburg 1954, 785–824. In an analogous fashion it is said of Jesus that he was similar to us in all things except sin. Misinterpreting this, some could retort that he was really not human, since to be human implies bondage and hence the capacity to sin!

9. The translation is by Barbara Stoler Miller, *The Bhagavad-Gita: Krishna's Counsel in Time of War*, New York and London 1986.

Paschal Mystery from a Philippine Perspective

Mary John Mananzan

Introduction

The paschal mystery is at the heart of the Hebrew-Christian faith. From the proto-experience of the deliverance of the Chosen People from the bondage of Egypt and their entry into the Promised Land, the Exodus theme runs through the history of salvation: an ever-recurring passover from slavery to freedom, from Good Friday to Easter Sunday, from suffering to glory, from death to life. This paper will reflect on how Filipino Christians in different stages of their history have allowed this mystery to mould their lives and influence their actions.

1. Historical background

Christianity came to the Philippines in the context of Spanish colonization in the sixteenth century through the triumph of the sword and the cross. Having no highly structured and highly developed religion which flourished in neighbouring countries, the inhabitants of the islands embraced Christianity.

However, the people have never really assimilated the religion and would resort to their own rituals in time of dire need. They had a cosmic religiosity which pervaded all the aspects of their life to such an extent that they clung to it in their deepest existential experiences and superimposed on it the new religion brought to them by their colonizers.

After three and a half centuries of Spanish rule, the islands came under the American régime when Spain ceded the Philippines to the United States following its defeat in the Spanish-American War in 1898. The Filipinos experienced another brand of Christianity, namely Protestantism.

To date, the sixty-three million inhabitants are divided into 85% Catholics, 6% Protestants, 4% Muslims; the rest still hold their ancient beliefs or profess no faith at all.

2. The Spanish legacy: the suffering Christ

When Filipinos see for the first time the *Pasos* in Seville during Holy Week, when the statues of Jesus and Mary are brought in procession throughout the city, they feel very much at home, because the Spanish missionaries brought a lot of religious practices of their homeland to their colonies.

One of the most important of these practices is the observance of Holy Week, especially the reading of the Passion Narrative (*Pasyon*) and the re-enactment of the sufferings and death of Christ. This was used not only as a catechetical means to teach the people but to attract them to the town from their scattered dwellings in the hillsides.

According to Nick Tiongson, these were used by the Spanish colonizers 'to inculcate among the Indios loyalty to Spain and Church . . . ; they encouraged resignation to things as they were and instilled preoccupation with morality and the afterlife rather than with conditions in this world'.

Rey Ileto, although accepting Nick Tiongson's contention, points out another function which the *Pasyon* developed: 'The second function, which probably was not intended by the friars, was to provide lowland Philippine society with a language for articulating its own values, ideals, and even hopes of liberation.'[1]

The people drew from the *Pasyon* much of the language of anti-colonialism in the late nineteenth century and shaped the ideals of the *Confradias* (religious brotherhoods) and inspired some of the uprisings of these millenaristic movements in the later part of the Spanish rule and in the early part of the colonial period. Ileto elaborates:

Even if we, for the moment, limit our attention to the *Pasyon Pilapil* as a text, its bearing on popular movements and social unrest can already be seen. For one thing, the inclusion of episodes relating to the Creation of the World, the Fall of Man (*sic*), and the Last Judgment makes the *Pasyon Pilapil* an image of universal history, the beginning and end of time, rather than a simple gospel story. In its narration of Christ's suffering, death and resurrection, and of the Day of Judgment, it provides powerful images of transition from one stage or era to another, e.g. darkness to light, despair to hope, misery to salvation, death to life, ignorance to knowledge, dishonour to purity, and so forth. During the

Spanish and American colonial eras, these images nurtured an undercurrent of millennial beliefs, which, in times of economic and political crisis, enabled the peasantry to take action under the leadership of individuals or groups promising deliverance from oppression. One of these groups, as we shall see, heralded the country's passage from the dark, miserable, dishonourable age of Spanish rule to a glowing era of freedom (18–19).

The Spanish legacy seems to have given a great emphasis to the first pole of the paschal mystery, namely the suffering rather than the glory, Good Friday rather than Easter Sunday. In a survey of the preferred image of Christ among grassroots Filipino, that of the crucified Christ came first (52%). The researcher Fr Benigno Beltran explains this preference:

> In a country where poverty, deprivation and oppression are the common lot of the masses, where typhoons and earthquakes frequently occur, it is not surprising that the image of the Crucified One, head bowed, mouth agape in excruciating agony, provides consolation and an outlet for pent-up emotions of sympathy and tragedy for the ignorant and the heavy-laden. For some, the sight of their crucified God increases the resolve to survive. The Cross is an essential part of Christian faith. The image of the Crucified provides a clear and unified image of how God responds to our most tangible reality – our being sinners. In the sight of the cross, Christians live in acceptance and trust in the suffering God who remains faithful in his love for sinful human beings.[2]

This emphasis on the suffering Christ is corroborated by the anthropologist Fr Frank Lynch, who writes: 'The Christ of the Filipinos is pre-eminently a suffering Christ. He is the beaten, scourged, humiliated and defeated Christ.'[3] In the same vein, James Ebner FSC comments on the omission of the resurrection in the Quiapo devotion to the Black Nazarene:

> The omission seems characteristic of the whole Filipino Catholicism. A look at Holy Week traditions can tell a lot of the story. No matter what clergy today may be saying to the crowds about the importance of Easter, nearly every parishioner you speak with has spent his/her religious energy by Good Friday night. The main event, plainly, is over. Even for so-called educated Filipinos, Easter apparently comes as a supplement, maybe even as an inconvenience. It seems safe to say that the deep-down faith of adult Filipinos is strongly a Calvary Catholicism.[4]

2. The paschal mystery in Filipino popular religiosity

Long after the Spaniards had left the Philippines, the religious practices they introduced remained. With characteristic ingenuity the Filipinos incorporated these into their daily lives and in some cases combined their ancient beliefs with these practices.

To this day, in many rural parishes the *Pasyon* is sung uninterruptedly for three days by old women. In some places young men make superficial blade cuts on their backs and proceed to flagellate themselves or let someone else whip them. This flagellation takes places in a sort of procession of these young men all over the town, and the procession ends in the river where they immerse themselves in the water. This is done as a fulfilment of vows they have made for certain intentions. In some other places some actually have themselves crucified with nails and all.

In a study of popular religious practices, a lay theologian, José de Mesa, points to some mention of the resurrection in what seems to be a predominantly Good Friday spirituality. For example, in a famous practice called the Moriones festival in the province of Marinduque, the *Pasyon* does not end with the death of Christ but with the testimony of the legendary soldier, Longhino, who pierced the side of Jesus, and whose blind eye was supposed to have been cured by the blood and water that flowed from Christ's side. The words put into his mouth as a testimony are a daring statement that Jesus has risen:

> Great Pilate, my eyes have seen Jesus rising from the dead. An angel descended and rolled back the stone. The face of the angel was blinding as lightning and his garment as white as snow. Nor was I the only one who saw the angel. All of us there were surprised and scared. Some of the Jewish sentries became dumb. When Jesus came out of the grave we saw that his face was as bright as the morning sun . . . ask the other centurions who were there. They too were witnesses to the resurrection of Christ.[5]

The enactment of the joyful meeting of Jesus and Mary on Holy Saturday is also found in all regions of the Philippines. This is called *Padafung* in Ibanag, *Domingo-sabet* in Ilocano, *Abet-abet* in Pangasinan, *Pasko ng salubong* in Pampanga, *Alleluya* in Bicol, and *Sugat* in the Visayas. Whatever it is called or whatever variation is introduced, the main movements are a procession of the men following the statue of Christ and a procession of women following the *Mater Dolorosa* (suffering mother). The two processions wind through separate routes around the town, but they enter two separate gates of the patio simultaneously. The principal angel (a dream role of all ten-year-old girls) then proceeds to change the black veil of the Virgin to blue to signify the end of her mourning.

De Mesa finds some problems in the understanding of resurrection as depicted in the religious practices just cited. In Filipino the word is translated as *muling pagkabuhay*, which literally means 'being alive again'. There is an impression that Jesus' resurrection is a return of Jesus to his former life in space and time. De Mesa feels that there is a catechetical, pedagogical need to present the resurrection as radical transformation into something totally new, into 'another, new, unparalleled, definitive immortal life – something utterly different' (125). His suggestion is to take the two Filipino concepts *hiya* (shame) to characterize the death on the cross and *dangal* (dignity and honour) to signify the resurrection. De Mesa explains:

> We have seen how the dignity and honour of Jesus was violated through the rejection and violent death on the cross. If this is so, then the resurrection must have something to say about Jesus, his message, his behaviour, his fate. Moreover, it has also something to say to us who claim to be followers of this rejected and shamed one.
>
> The resurrection message reveals the very thing that was not to be expected: that this crucified Jesus, despite everything, was right. God took the side of the one who had totally committed himself to him, who gave his life for the cause of God and human beings . . .
>
> The resurrection means that Jesus' claim, his faith in God's closeness, his obedience, his freedom, his joy, his whole action and suffering were confirmed.

In the context of Filipino culture where dignity and honour and shame are important concepts, and in a situation where human dignity is continuously trampled upon in the name of progress and national security, to speak of the resurrection in this way gives it significance and relevance. And wherever this dignity is restored or struggled for, there the resurrection is experienced anew.

4. The paschal mystery in the theology of struggle

It is significant that Filipino theologians who have been inspired by liberation theology prefer to have their theology called theology of struggle rather than liberation theology. It is not so much a theology about struggle but in the context of struggle – the struggle of the great majority of the Filipino people for justice. It emphasizes the peoples' own effort to work out their liberation amidst centuries of oppression and injustice. Lester

Edwin Ruiz gives another explanation for the name taking the biblical tradition of Jacob wrestling (struggling with God). He writes:

> In the biblical tradition, it is said that God and Jacob wrestled all night. God dislocated Jacob's hip, but Jacob would not let go. As a result of their struggle, God saw that this man had become a radically new man. Therefore, the story goes, God changed this man's name from Jacob, which means 'may God protect', to Israel, which means at one and the same time 'He who struggles with God' or 'God struggles' (Halpem, 1986). This is a struggle that is at once personal, political, historical, sacred. But precisely because it is all of this, it must always be incomplete, always done 'on the run', always a servant of the larger struggle for transformation.[6]

Ed dela Torre, who may be considered the father of the theology of struggle, was the first one who said that the Filipino theology we need today is a theology of struggle, rather than a theology of liberation. This is not to denigrate the theology of liberation but, as Fely Carino paraphrases dela Torre's stand: 'While it remains important to stay within the ambit of the theological mode represented by the theology of liberation, it is nevertheless necessary that in our situation we pay more attention to the "means" by which "liberation" as an end may be attained.'[7]

Reminiscent of the paschal mystery, in 1972 Ed dela Torre wrote an article on the 'Passion, Death and Resurrection of the Petty-Bourgeois Christian'.[8] He traces the gradual awakening of the Christians to the oppressive situation at the outbreak of martial law in 1972 and the emerging of the forces of resistance. The Filipino middle-class Christian faced the challenge of either just watching the militant forces go by, being an obstacle to them, or joining them. But there were dilemmas. How does one honestly claim to be Christian while choosing to work along lines that are rejected by other Christians as atheistic, materialistic and violent? Ed dela Torre, identifying himself with the petty-bourgeois Christian, expresses their ambivalence:

> . . . we crucified ourselves on a cross of our own making, wanting to love, to serve the people, but always holding back because we might be used, because it might violate our principles and so we loved 'pure and chaste from afar'. Virgins who loved too wisely but not too well, afraid to risk, waiting for immaculate conceptions and virgin births of plans, organizations, movements, societies (p. 95).

Humbled by the truth about themselves, some petty-bourgeois Christians freed themselves from impossible dreams of being the leaders of the people but accepted the role of being of service to the basic masses. Some had to die in a sense – by defecting from the establishments they used to serve. Some even had to die in a more literal sense when they joined the armed struggle. But dela Torre points out a more radical death: 'The Christian is faced with an even more frightening death. His God dies. The God who revealed social principles and performed miracles of power is suddenly challenged by the power of people who try to make history' (96). But what about the resurrection? Where is the new petty-bourgeois and the new Christianity? There is a new consciousness emerging. There is a redefinition of one's faith. But there is still a long way to go. Dela Torre concludes:

> In the meantime it is Lent and, wandering through the desert, one sometimes looks back wistfully at the secure definitions one has left and remembers with some vacillation the theological, political and economic fleshpots of the establishment. And grumbles at leaders and companions, and thinks of repentance and struggle and hopes that the fight to level the hills and fill up the valleys will prepare the way for the coming Kingdom (97).

Carlos Abesamis, a biblical theologian, takes his starting point from the first passover, the exodus of the chosen people from Egypt. He considers this as 'the central event in the Israelitic salvation history'. In this event the God of history works out a salvation among the chosen people that is both total and concrete: total in the sense of affecting the whole person, body and soul, and having a societal context rather than being merely individualistic and concrete because the Israelites were liberated from concrete evils (slavery and oppression) and experienced concrete blessings (the promised land). The exodus event is therefore primarily a 'justice event', and because the exodus is the central event, 'the most primitive article of the faith is about justice and a God of justice'.[9] This concept of salvation, according to Abesamis, runs through the whole history of the Hebrew-Christian tradition.

Jesus himself upheld this concept of salvation. The phrase used by Jesus to signify salvation is the Reign of God, and the signs that this Reign of God had come were concrete blessings like the blind seeing, the lame walking, the lepers being cleansed.

The Hellenization of Christianity and other developments unfortunately narrowed down this idea of salvation into 'the salvation of the soul from sin, hell and death, in order to go to heaven'. This has made salvation individualistic, dualistic and other-worldly. The task of theologians is to recover the original meaning of salvation, where justice was central. Abesamis concludes: 'It is today's poor and their struggle that have challenged us to go back to our biblical roots and rediscover the gospel of justice and liberation in the very core of Jesus' original mission. May this gospel in turn help to fire us to dedicate ourselves to the task of justice and liberation in our time."[10]

5. Filipino feminist theology

Feminist theologians in the Philippines consider as the starting point of their theologizing the struggles of Filipino women for fuller humanity in the context of the overall struggle for societal transformation and total human liberation. In a country beset by poverty, hunger, natural calamities, foreign debt and 'total war', the women feel doubly oppressed. With the growing frustration of men comes also the greater frequency of cases of violence against women. The Western Police District of Metro Manila, for example, cites as the most frequent crime in its area 'the rape, robbery, and murder of a woman'. The economic crisis has also given rise to various forms of trafficking in women both in the domestic and foreign markets as prostitutes, mail-order brides and overseas workers. Truly it is the women who can best empathize with the suffering Christ.

However, it is in these very experiences that the seeds of women's liberation have begun. A women's movement has begun that has conscientized the women to see that it is only through their bonding that they can overcome their oppression, empower one another and work towards their liberation. They have pinpointed the cause of their triple burden of economic deprivation, gender exploitation and social victimization from the 'interrelated system of domination which feminists refer to as patriarchy'.[11] They have traced the introduction of Western patriarchy to the Spanish conquest of the Philippines, with the Spanish friars bent on domesticating the once free and socially active *mujer indigena*.

Following the flow of the paschal mystery, the feminist theologians see hope in their emancipatory struggle. They are even gradually developing a spirituality that seems to be a corrective to the Good-Friday religiosity of folk Catholicism in the country. In one of my articles, I characterize this spirituality thus:

It is a spirituality that is joyful rather than austere, active rather than passive, expansive rather than limiting. It celebrates rather than fasts; it surrenders rather than controls. It is an Easter rather than a Good Friday spirituality. It is creative rather than conservative . . . This emerging spirituality of women promises to be vibrant, liberating and colourful. Its direction and tendencies seem to open up to greater possibilities of life and freedom and therefore to more and more opportunities to be truly, intensely and wholly alive.[12]

Conclusion

We started with the claim that the paschal mystery is at the heart of the Hebrew-Christian faith. It is actually in the heart of life itself, because life is the continuous passover from darkness to light, from agony to ecstasy, from death to life. Filipino Christians have experienced in their history the predominance of darkness, agony and death, having undergone three and a half centuries of colonial rule and still experiencing the shackles of neo-colonialism, even after their country had gained its political independence. The people still suffer from economic crisis, political instability and cultural alienation. No wonder that Filipino spirituality is still a predominantly Good Friday spirituality. But there are signs of hope. A political consciousness and social movements for change have developed among its people that give the promise of an Easter Sunday.

Notes

1. Nick Tiongson, paraphrased in Rey Ileto, *Pasyon and Revolution*, Quezon City 1979, 16–17; Ileto's own words are on p. 15.
2. Benigno Beltran, *The Christology of the Inarticulate*, Manila 1987, 123.
3. F. Lynch, 'Catholicism', in *Area Handbook on the Philippines*, 1956, p. 662.
4. James Ebner, 'God: A Problem in Filipino Catholicism', *Vision* IV.1, 1978, 19.
5. José de Mesa, in *Solidarity with Culture*, Quezon City 1987, 106.
6. L. E. Ruiz, 'Towards a Theology of Politics', in *Theology, Politics and Struggle*, Quezon City 1986, 43–4.
7. Fely Carino, 'What About the Theology of Struggle?', in *Religion and Society*, Manila 1987, viii.
8. Edicio dela Torre, *Touching Ground, Taking Root*, Quezon City, 87–97.
9. Carlos Abesamis, *Exploring the Core of Biblical Faith*, Quezon City 1991, 30, 32.
10. Carlos Abesamis, 'Good News to the Poor', in *Religion and Society*, Manila 1987, 213.
11. EATWOT Women, *Patriarchy in Asia*, Manila 1991, 8.
12. Mary John Mananzan, 'Emerging Spirituality of Women', in *Essays on Women*, Manila 1987, 158.

Aspects of Christianity in Vietnam

Mai Thành

Prelude

In writing this article I have been unable to help reliving the solemn yet luminous drama which I have experienced with my family on our long way towards the light of faith in Jesus Christ. By way of a prelude, I shall recall some of the aspects of this way as a reflection and outline of what the Christians of Vietnam have undergone in their adherence to the Roman Catholic church.

It was the autumn of 1946. Dark clouds covered the sky of my country, broken here and there by the gloomy grumbling of cannons: it was the war between the French army and a Vietnam which had proclaimed its independence the previous autumn under the leadership of Hô Chi Minh, founder of Indo-Chinese Communism and President of the Democratic Republic of Vietnam. I was eighteen. Motivated by the certainty of finding the light of my life in Christ, I took the decision to ask my father for permission to receive Christian baptism.

'That's impossible,' my father replied, visibly shaken. 'If you want to remain my daughter, swear to me that you will never commit this impiety.'

I kept silent.

'If you are resolved to become a Catholic, we cannot live under the same roof. You have to choose: one of us will have to leave this house.'

I didn't dare to speak or move. Papa took his umbrella and went out of the house without saying a word.

Thirty years later, in the spring of 1980, my father, now weakened by age, was visited by a priest who was a great friend of my older brother. Quite unexpectedly, my father told the priest of his desire to become a Christian. Everyone was very moved. My father received baptism shortly afterwards. A month later, our elderly Confucian, aged eighty-five, was welcomed newborn into the kingdom of the eternal Father – an eternal Easter for our earthly father after a long fast spent with his children here below. At the funeral mass, my older brother paid the best homage of filial piety both to the Father of heaven and to his father here below by hailing the arrival on the eternal shore of this 'child of the twenty-fifth hour'!

What had happened between that autumn long ago and today's spring? A road dappled with shade and sunlight. In a way the echo of another great drama, the death and resurrection of a people, a church, that of Vietnam. So here is what happened, set in the history of the evangelization of this portion of humanity which occupies the eastern edge of the Indo-Chinese peninsula.

A situation at the crossroads

Vietnam is situated at the confluence of two oceans, the Indian Ocean and the Pacific Ocean. During the thirteenth, fourteenth and fifteenth centuries it was a port of call for navigators and Western merchants who were mapping out a route to the 'East Indies'. This was the route of silk, perfumes and spices, on which arms and merchandise crossed paths and sometimes clashed in tragic conflicts.

The coast of Vietnam was also a port of call at which missionaries on board Spanish and Portuguese ships stopped. Having come from their native land, or from Macacca, Macao or Manila, cities under the patronage of Portugal, they were the first zealous workers for the gospel in this land. The very first was Gaspard de Santa Cruz, and he was followed by others – Dominicans, Franciscans, Augustinians and other secular priests –between 1550 and 1560. Their first impressions of the people of the coast were most favourable: they found them open to the first seeds of the good news. So what was the human sphere these missionaries encountered?

The human context

Over the course of almost two millennia, the Vietnamese spirit has been steeped in cultural and religious values with roots on the one hand in Confucianism and Taoism deriving from China, and on the other in Buddhism originally from India, but arriving in Vietnam through the Chinese bonzes . . . Our people assimilated these values, adapting them to its own genius, and made them a cultural heritage which has lived on to our day, despite the great social and political upheavals that they have undergone over the course of centuries.

As with any other religion, these traditions certainly took deviant forms at a popular level, but they brought to Vietnamese society a polyvalent religious base in which Christianity was to find precious 'foundation stones' and happy harmonies:

From Confucianism we have received *a sense of the person, a sense of the family, a sense of the sacred, of God*.

1. *A sense of the person*: what has made human beings is the virtue of humanity which has constantly to be perfected. As Confucius says, 'Let the good man see in his neighbour the vision of himself; that is the sure way of perfection. This humanity is the foundation of universal love, since beyond the four oceans all men are brothers.'

2. *A sense of the family*: the good man studies the root of things. If he has found the root, his way will flourish – a way understood in the sense of virtue, habitual conduct, religion. And the root of good is respect for father, mother and elders. It is filial piety, a virtue which embraces all other virtues and inspires and governs all human acts. Those who perfect themselves intellectually and morally to honour their parents and improve the body, soul and life which their parents have given them, are on the way. Thanks to that they will bring order to the family before being able to govern the country and pacify the world.

3. *A sense of God*: while not seeing this in explicit terms, Confucius has the intuition of a creator God, a supreme being, providence, justice, goodness. The worship that human beings must offer to God is expressed in their practical conduct in accordance with the ethics mentioned above: it is in the degree to which the noble man honours God and his ancestors that he shows himself benevolent towards his neighbour and maintains harmony between heaven and earth. This cosmic vision of human beings as those who provide a union between the power of Heaven and life on earth, to some degree and without knowing it, evokes the mediating role of Christ between his Father in heaven and his brothers on pilgrimage along earthly ways.

This sense of harmony is also expressed by the Confucian through the virtues of the 'just environment', of tolerance, moderation, civility and fidelity.

From Taoism we receive the notion of a transcendent God, the Tao, the supreme way, an ineffable, unfathomable Beyond which generates all being and is humble because it does not impose itself. Thus Lao-tse: 'Benevolent, it nourishes all being without imposing on them as a master. Because of its constant disinterestedness, it is like a diminished being. However, all beings flow towards it because of its liberality and it finds itself increased. The wise man who imitates this humble and generous principle also makes himself small.'

Buddhism, the religion which is most widespread in Vietnam both among kings and literati and among the people, teaches detachment, universal compassion, non-violence, respect for life, benevolence and disinterestedness. The Pali Canon expresses the teaching of the Buddha like this: 'Monks, just as in the last month of the season of rains in autumn the sun, rising in a cloudless sky, banishes all darkness with its rays of splendour, so all the means employed to obtain a religious merit do not have the value of a sixth of benevolence. Benevolence, deliverance of the heart, absorbs them, makes them shine and gleams in radiant splendour.'

Among the rectitudes which make up the Eightfold Path, Buddha explains right contemplation like this:

A monk always respects his body and leads an active, reflective, contemplative life, having detached himself from pleasure and pain; he respects his sensations, and leads an active, reflective, contemplative life, having detached himself from pleasure and pain; he respects his spirit, and leads an active, reflective, contemplative life, having detached himself from pleasure and pain; he respects the elements of life, and leads an active, reflective, contemplative life, having detached himself from pleasure and pain. That, monks, is the rectitude of contemplation.

How do the Vietnamese people integrate these three religions (summed up here as simply as possible) in their life?

Endowed with a natural and quite practical religious sense, Vietnamese believers are not embarrassed by dogmas or by rational confrontations between the different ethics. Confucian in family and in social relationships, they practise Buddhist fasting, meditate on the Sutras, go to the pagoda or withdraw as hermits in the face of the evil which corrupts individuals and society, in accordance with the spirit of Taoist detachment. This religious syncretism is developed and expressed by a fundamental conciliatory tolerance: all the religions are good, since they only seek human well-being. So in the schools and universities the timetable offers students all three religions, without discrimination or critical comparison. These religions, like all human quests, certainly have their imperfections. But beyond question a synthesis of these complementary religious values constitutes the religious foundation of the people of this country, and has prepared well-tilled and fertile soil for the germination of the Christian faith. This is what many missionaries have noticed throughout the work of Christian preaching.

According to the Jesuit Alexander of Rhodes, an eminent missionary to Vietnam whom I shall be describing later, 'this country was a fertile land on which Heaven poured its dew and in which all the fields bear all kinds of fruit in abundance' (an extract from the accounts of his travels, which are well-known in Vietnam).

Another missionary and anthropologist, Fr Cadieu, in his studies on the religious beliefs and practices of the Vietnamese, pertinently remarks that 'among the Vietnamese and in all classes of society, religious feeling is manifested in a powerful way and dominates the whole of life; it envelops with the tight nets of its practices the most important and the most humble daily actions'.[1]

The dawn of evangelization

After periodic and temporary stays by the first evangelists on the coast of the country, a Spanish priest, Ordonnez de Cevallos, landed in Tonkin – in the north of the country – in 1590. The history of these beginnings notes that in eight months his preaching reached many members of the royal family. The ruler's sister, Princess Mai Hoa, was baptized Maria Flora, and was so won over by the gospel that she asked permission to found a monastery, of which she became superior. The ground had been opened up. Other missionaries came, Jesuits expelled from Japan or sent from Macao, the latter including Frs Pierre Marquez and Alexander of Rhodes. The latter, of Provençal origin and extremely gifted in languages, rapidly mastered Vietnamese. He was also strong in mathematics and astronomy. He gained the friendship of the lord of Hanoi and succeeded in opening a church in 1627. There he preached for between four and six hours a day. At Christmas, a great crowd came to hear him speak of 'Jesus Christ made man'. Later he spoke in these terms: 'The fruit was so great as to be almost unbelievable. A sister of the king and seventeen of her entourage, along with famous captains, were baptized. In three years the number reached 3500. Nothing was more surprising than the ease I found in converting the "priests of idols" who are ordinarily the most obstinate; I baptized 200 of them, and they then helped us considerably in converting the others.'[2]

Whether or not these figures are accurate, the undeniable fact is the profound attraction that people at different levels felt for the gospel message.

A road of light dappled with shade

The season of good harvests lasted almost three years. Orders banning

Christianity and expelling the missionaries were given by the rulers and men of letters in the face of the rapid expansion of the nuclei of Christianity. The main reasons for this were:

1. The obligation on the converts to abandon the cult of ancestors, which was considered idolatry and superstition. The offering of food on the altar dedicated to the dead and prostrations before this altar were prohibited by the missionaries. The same went for the ceremonies of prayer before Buddha. But above all it was the ban on expressing filial piety before the altar of the ancestors which caused the most discontent. This ban was to last until the twentieth century, through the papal constitutions *Ex illa die* (1715) and *Ex quo singulari* (1742) on the question of the famous 'rites dispute'.

These measures stemmed from the doctrinal intransigence of the Catholic church after the Council of Trent, dogged by the fear of schism and a very marked dualistic concept which separated church and the world, soul and body, heaven and the terrestrial city, and Christianity and other religions, which were deemed to be 'pagan' or 'diabolical'. This discrimination against religious values which were often also secular in the East, as in Vietnam, was the origin of persecutions and martyrdoms over the centuries.

Furthermore, the ban on polygamy caused a good deal of trouble in families – husbands were obliged to send away wives to whom they had long been married – and in addition there were totally new customs: converts had incomprehensible names (baptismal names) and wore an unknown object – the cross – around their necks, and so on.

2. The hatred of the rulers of the country for the missionaries because of their links with the Western merchants. Transported in the ships of the merchants and going side by side with them, often defended by their flag, the messengers of the gospel were either received with good grace or rejected, depending on the fluctuations of relationships between the kings and the foreign navigators. From the sixteenth to the eighteenth century Vietnam was divided, the North governed by the Trinh lords and the south by the Nguyen. The rivalry between these two often led to armed conflicts. As the Portuguese ships brought munitions to both sides and the missionaries utilized these deliveries to speak of religion, the missionaries were often identified with foreign enemies. Thus the cross brought by the evangelists was thought of as 'the Portuguese flag'. Some believed that 'the Portuguese would readily come with their best merchandise wherever they saw this flag'.

In addition to the preaching of the gospel, a very important contribution by the missionary Alexander of Rhodes was the Romanization of

Vietnamese script, which hitherto had been written in Chinese characters with a complicated ideographic structure. Alexander, anticipated by others, had the idea of using the European alphabet for transcribing the phonemes, adding diacritical signs to express the tones of Vietnamese speech. The first two works in this new script were a milestone in history: *The Catechism for Those who Want to Receive Baptism, Explained in Eight Days*, and *The Annamite-Portuguese-Latin Dictionary*. They were the work of Alexander of Rhodes. This invention allowed a rapid dissemination not only of the good news but also of Vietnamese literature in society. Perfected some time later, this script still remains our national script, the *quôć ngũ*.

Growth and efforts to put down roots.

The first Christian communities founded by the Jesuits grew quite quickly, despite the ups and downs caused by social problems. The fervour of the newly-converted was a great stimulus for the workers of the kingdom. To meet the new needs of growing Christianity, in 1659 Rome sent the two first French vicars apostolic, Mgr François Palu for Tonkin and Mgr Lambert de La Motte for Cochin-China. The Roman recommendations called for the following:

> training of indigenous priests and even bishops;
> obedience to Rome;
> abstinence from political involvement;
> respect for local civilizations and customs.

'Avoid any attempt and any advice to these people to make them change their rites, their customs and their morals, provided that they are not manifestly contrary to religion. In fact there is nothing more absurd than to introduce France, Spain or Italy to the Chinese. That is not what you should introduce, but the faith, which does not reject nor damage either liturgies or customs, provided that they are not bad; on the contrary, faith wants them to be protected' (Decree of the Congregation of Faith, under Pope Alexander VIII).

Missionary work then took on a new lease of life with the formation of indigenous priests, communities of catechists and the first religious congregation in the country, the Lovers of the Cross. These last were responsible for pastoral work, including visits to Christian communities who had no priests. Their role was very important in periods of repression: leading prayers, preaching in place of priests, visiting and looking after the sick, the distribution of communion, the baptism of children, re-education of women.

The combined effort of the priests of the foreign missions of Paris, and the Spanish Jesuits, Franciscans and Dominicans, established Christianity on a more solid basis. The number of Catholics is estimated at between 200,000 and 300,000. Despite the difficulties encountered in the formation of priests (periodical bans on preaching, the laborious task of learning Latin, poverty), the first seminary was established on a junk moored off Faifoo, in the centre of Vietnam. In 1668, four priests were ordained, two for the north and two others for the south.

Unfortunately persecution resumed, aggravated by dissensions among the church authorities: problems of jurisdiction, a statute dividing pastoral areas between secular and religious priests coming from different countries with different missionary perspectives, and so on.

The intervention of France

In addition to the difficulties indicated earlier, the eighteenth century added other obstacles to evangelization. In 1750 a French commercial expedition led by a merchant collapsed. The lord of the south, irritated with him, expelled foreigners, had places of worship destroyed and severely punished the Catholics. The persecuted church bravely continued to live out its faith through the squalls. The number of priests reached twenty-five in the north.

The civil war between the lords became more complicated towards the end of the eighteenth century as a result of the rebellion of the Tay Son in the southern centre of the country. After annihilating the lords of both north and south, Nguyên Huê proclaimed himself emperor (1778–1792). A last survivor of the lords of the south named Nguyên Anh recruited an army to defeat Nguyên Huê and reconquer the kingdom. He sought the military aid of France through Bishop Pigneau de Béhaine, vicar apostolic of the south. After hesitations and fruitless approaches to other Western countries interested in the East, the bishop had himself made Nguyên Anh's ambassador to the king of France. The success was only apparent. Pigneau de Béhaine returned two years later with the young prince, son of Nguyên Anh, who had been entrusted to him in this diplomatic manoeuvre. Some traders and volunteers joined the ambassador-priest to go to Cochin-China. The Tay Son thereupon unleashed bloody persecutions against the Christians. But the bishop's desire to enjoy more religious freedom through the aid he brought to Nguyên Anh was realized on the accession of the latter, who became

King Gia Long in 1802. Peace was restored to the reunified country and the Catholics had more freedom.

A new storm

After the death of Gia Long in 1820, the religion of Vietnam entered a violent storm of persecutions under the successive reigns of kings Minh Mang Thiêu Tri and Tu Duc. The edicts against 'the religion of the Europeans which corrupts men's hearts' prompted both by the arrival of warships and 'alien Christian customs' led to fearful persecutions. Priests, both foreign and Vietnamese, and laity loyal to their faith, succumbed to cruel torture and execution. Tens of thousands of Christians were massacred between 1880 and 1884.

The punishment from France made the situation worse and ended up in the conquest of Vietnam, which began in 1857–8.

Under French colonization

Despite the muted local revolts, this period of the absence of war and persecution allowed Christianity to consolidate and saw the development of seminaries, the birth of diocesan women's religious congregations and the foundation of men's and women's congregations, both apostolic and contemplative, which originated above all in France. The growth of schools, colleges, hospitals and welfare centres had a great influence on both Christian and non-Christian milieus. Even more than by direct preaching, evangelization through education and social service silently and profoundly put its stamp on the Vietnamese consciousness, giving rise to conversions and religious vocations with an amazing fervour. Christian humanism, rationalistic science, art and philosophy conveyed through schools and universities, represents an important contribution to the development of Vietnamese society.

The establishment of the original Catholic hierarchy of the country, the consecration of its first three bishops – Nguyên Ba Tong (1933), Hô Noc Cân (1935) and Ngô Dinh Thuc (1938) – delighted Christians throughout the land. In 1940 they numbered 1.5 million out of a population of 18 million, with almost 1000 Vietnamese priests and 300 French missionaries.

Towards national independence

The Japanese *coup d'état* on 9 March 1945 caused a break in the French presence. The autumn of the same year saw the proclamation of national independence by Hô Chi Minh. The French army returned in 1946, to engage in a war which was terminated by the Geneva agreement in 1954, after the French defeat. This agreement divided the country into two states, Communist in the north and nationalist in the south. There was a massive emigration of Christians southwards, which robbed the North of an important part of its evangelical vigour. For those who remained, this was a period of shadowy conflicts in which Marxist ideology and patriotism were in confrontation or absorbed into each other, in which Christians were called 'reactionaries' because they refused all collaboration with the government. Since the Communists were themselves deemed 'intrinsically perverse' by Rome, the pastoral letter of the hierarchy in 1951, proclaimed by an apostolic nuncio of foreign origin, excommunicated any Catholic who collaborated in any way with the Communists. Some bishops refused the sacraments to parents who sent their children to public schools, the only ones existing under the Communist régime. The church of the North lived or survived in extreme difficulties. In some places it became a bastion of resistance and a ghetto walled in on itself.

South Vietnam experienced calm until 1960, though it could not escape the conflicts inherent in the complex situation of the country. In 1960 the church had its Vietnamese hierarchy with three archdioceses in the north, centre and south, under the papacy of John XXIII. However, the most important event was the application of the decree *Plane compertum est* to Vietnam, under Paul VI, in 1965. This authorized ancestor worship in families of Christian converts. The ban on the sacred duty of filial piety which had lasted four centuries had at last been lifted. The church began to restore to Confucian families their 'lost' children, after so many family, political and social conflicts and martyrdoms. This was also the date when my brothers, sisters and I rejoined the family to celebrate the cult of our ancestors in the presence of our Confucian father. Before the altar that we had deserted twenty years ago we were deeply moved to combine our piety with that of our father for intense communion with the beyond, a kingdom which, though invisible, is real. A joyful meal followed to celebrate the return of the 'prodigal' children. My father concluded: 'The West has come nearer to the East and Christianity to our great ancestral traditions. If this integration is understood and applied everywhere, it will have a beneficial influence on the people.' Since then we have sought to express our filial piety on all favourable occasions, not only by cultic actions but by that openness to human values which has been encouraged by Vatican II, in particular by *Gaudium et Spes*, *Lumen Gentium* and *Nostra Aetate*. That explains the radiant ending of our family drama which I mentioned at the beginning of this article: the happy encounter between our earthly father and the Father of heaven.

National unification under the Communist régime: co-existence, conflict or dialogue?

The year 1975, which saw the end of the complex war between South and North Vietnam, supported by the Americans on the one hand and the Socialist bloc on the other, posed a new challenge to the church of Vietnam: confrontation with Marxist-Leninist ideology. There was fear, anguish, antagonism, exodus abroad, discrimination and mistrust within the country and within the Catholic church. But the divergence in positions did not prevent a number of Christians, and the hierarchy with them, from seeking a way of reconciliation and dialogue. The pastoral letter of the bishops in 1980 marked a new mentality:

> The church is journeying with all humanity, joining its hopes and sufferings to those of the people (*Gaudium et Spes* 40.2). That is why we must journey with our people, sharing with them a community of destiny, since our country is the sphere in which God calls us to live as his children. Our country is the motherland which has conceived us in our journey towards the vocation of being children of God. Our people is the community which God has entrusted to us to serve as earthly citizens and as members of the people of God.

In their communications within the country and abroad, men and women religious affirmed that their presence in this country was *an option for the gospel*, convinced that 'human beings are the fundamental route for the church' and that the Vietnamese salvation history has to be realized in the process of the history of its people. So despite the inevitable suspicions rooted in a long conflict which was both socio-cultural and political, Christians, men and especially women religious, that mobile labour force which can operate in any terrain, hastened towards the most urgent tasks of reconstructing the ravaged country and above all binding up the deep wounds bequeathed by history. The way of reconciliation is open; that of dialogue must advance at all levels and with all the world. Catholics are aware of being the leaven of humanity, the ferment of love, joy and hope, witnesses to a servant and poor church, in the image of their Master in the kenosis of incarnation.

What perspectives for the future?

In its immense effort to survive and live in loyalty to its faith at the heart of the tormented history of its people, the church of Vietnam has not yet been able to live in symbiosis with the culture for which it was born. It still keeps a Western costume and garb in its liturgy, its dogmatic concepts shaped by a foreign culture, an imported mental and material architecture. These elements are indubitably the riches of millennia which we too have welcomed and recognized. But Christ's robe of many colours must also be woven with silk threads from the East and from Vietnam. The face of Christ in this country must be incarnated more in its culture, its quest for bread and dignity and for true freedom.

So far there have certainly been laudable efforts on the part of the Catholics of our country in certain areas: liturgical hymns expressed with the instruments and music of the country, some reviews, theological or spiritual essays, attempts – still timid – at dialogue with Buddhism, the translation of the Bible and the Breviary into the vernacular, a new catechism adapted to the situation which is still undergoing trial. But these efforts are still very limited because of more urgent preoccupations with the profound social and political changes; that is also the cause of the absence of organs for research and forward-looking reflection.

What are the possible directions for a catechesis and a theology which are more incarnated in the fabric of Vietnamese culture and experience? Since I have no theological competence, I would prefer to suggest some elements drawn from my own experience as a Vietnamese woman converted to the gospel and in the course of being converted to the calls of the Christ of today.

1. *The filial dimension of human beings*. Is not filial piety, that basic virtue which cannot be uprooted from the Vietnamese heart, a certain reflection of that other filial piety, both divine and human, lived out by the only-begotten Son of God before the eternal Father from whom he issued and to whom he returned? Is not the Gospel of St John the unfolding of time and space in human history of this substantive filiality which binds his being to that of the Father?

> 'I have come down from heaven, not to do my own will, but the will of him who sent me' (John 6.38).
> 'For this is the will of my Father, that every one who sees the Son and believes in him should have eternal life' (6.40).
> 'My food is to do the will of him who sent me, and to accomplish his work' (4.34).
> 'I do as the Father has commanded me, so that the world may know that I love the Father' (14.31).

One could go even deeper into this filial piety, consummated on the cross: 'Father, into your hands I commend my spirit' (Luke 23.46).

It was in the movement of this unsurpassable filiality of Jesus on the cross that on the day of the celebration of the cult of my ancestors in my family, after the publication of *Plane compertum est*, standing before the family altar, I entered into communion with the 'firstborn from among all creation', older brother and priest of the universe. The first word of prayer which rose to my heart was 'Our Father, who art in heaven'. The rest was simply thanksgiving to the supreme Father from whom all fatherhood here below derives.

2. *Brothers and sisters and the family dimension*. Since the Vietnamese family is the heart of all relationships, the relationships that we weave with our compatriots express these relationships in our everyday language. The little that we know of ourselves, we express in terms of kinship, so when I am talking to people of my parents' age, instead of calling them *ong* (sir) or *bà* (madam) I call them *bác* or *chú* (uncle), *thím* or *cô* (aunt). Those of the age of my brothers and sisters become *anh*, *chi* or *em*, depending on whether they are a little older or younger than I am. I also do the same thing with those of the age of my grandparents, great uncles, and so on. Here is an example: the ex-President Hô Chi Minh has continued to be called 'Uncle Hô' in the written rendering of the spoken language of the country. This is quite proper to the Vietnamese mentality and language, since unlike the French and Germans, and like the English and Americans, the Chinese and other neighbouring peoples use 'I' or 'you' without any other connotations of affection or kinship.

I deliberately use this distinctive language in my everyday encounters: with someone working in a shop, pedalling a cycle-taxi, or my colleague at the office. In this way I attempt a sisterly approach which is open to other deeper values. Why not, I ask myself, rely on this psychology to develop and Christianize the sense of evangelical kinship founded on our filiality towards God the Father, through his Son our older brother and Mary our mother?

It seems to me that this sense of the family, rooted in the Vietnamese heart, can easily fit into the generative movement of the divine family, each of whose members is defined in relationships to the others: Father, Son, Spirit. Do not all the families gathered and restored here by the Son into a new humanity and universal family stem from this original family? Christ did not come to abolish but to fulfil.

3. *A dimension of dialogue*. Dialogue is a movement towards the other. The other can be someone like, different or opposed. Though difficult, our experience with our Communist compatriots has been possible and is bearing fruit. This is a dialogue which does not operate at the level of words or discussion, but is a dialogue of friendship, co-operation, shared work in

the service of all. This dialogue inspires us to dialogue with others: with those of other religions and beliefs, other cultures, other options, other people, a dialogue founded on the dialogue of incarnation achieved by the Son of God. It presupposes a kenosis, the basis for all reconciliation, for the harmony of contraries, the encounter of extremes.

The church of Vietnam is called to enter into this divine-human movement by going out of itself, stripping itself further of all that encumbers it and removes it from the people it seeks to serve. Instead of defending itself in the name of the church 'which alone serves the truth', it is making itself encounter, openness, sharing, in respect and understanding for the other. Far from thinking that 'outside the church there is no salvation' and singing 'Christus vincit, Christus regnat, Christus imperat', often at inopportune moments, it is attempting to model itself on the Beatitudes and the Servant Songs, on this 'Wholly Other' who has become one like us, the partner, the brother, the intimate friend, the spouse. To join this 'Wholly Other' I need the other. A French missionary who became an anthropologist as a result of his mission to the ethnic tribes on the high plateau of Vietnam put it like this:

> We must listen to the Amen of the people (amen according to their own language, their own mentality) . . . God was there and I did not know it. When I meet the atheist or the pagan I am confronted with the image of God, I am on holy ground. One takes off one's shoes and approaches quietly. If I made a noise by talking too loudly, I would deafen his religious sense and would not hear that imperceptible palpitation in him which waits for the liberating revelation. Does God act any differently with me? Does he overwhelm me by making me see everything all at once? God is there, but allows himself to be sought, step by step, to prepare for the meeting.[3]

Conclusion

After more than four centuries of evangelization, how is the church in Vietnam living out its faith today? All the foreign visitors who have come to Vietnam in the last five years have been struck by its growing vigour, despite the difficulties inherent in the great social and political changes in the country. 'Vietnam, a Church of Astonishing Vitality', was the title of an article which Fr Albert Longchamp wrote in *Témoignage Chrétien* of 14 March 1988. Here is an incomplete summary:

Proportion of Catholics: 8–9% of the population;

Number of bishops: 32 for 35 dioceses (5 bishops who have died have
not been replaced);
Religious: 5100;
Priests: 1782;
Seminarians: 557 (the number is low in relation to the demand from
candidates);
Number of baptisms in Ho Chi Minh City in 1991 : 3406 (more than half
are adult baptisms).

These figures will increase, thanks to the dialogue between church and
state. Mutual understanding and openness now offer wider scope for
education and social service. Christians, religious and priests are aware of
their historical responsibility, trying to assimilate the past and open up new
ways for the future. They have the conviction that their faith, whether
flowing in silence in subterranean springs or emerging into the light of day
through their living testimony, will contribute to making the ricefields of
Vietnam and the fields of Christ's church flourish. Through the ruptures
and discontinuities in human history they can discern the continuing
framework of the history of salvation. They go humbly but joyfully at the
heart of their people, side by side with this 'stranger' on the way to
Emmaus, until the bread is broken. That is why they march on, wiping off
their sweat, with a smile of love and hope on their lips.

Translated by John Bowden

Notes

1. Quoted by Nguyen Huy Lai in *La tradition religieuse, spirituelle et sociale du Viet
Nam: sa confrontation avec le christianisme*, Paris 1981, 40.
2. Quoted by Guy Marie Oury in *Le Viet Nam des martyrs des saints*, Paris 1988,
25.
3. Jacques Dournes, *L'offrande des peuples*, Paris 1967, 4.

Other documents
Claude Lange, 'Histoire du christianisme', in *Viet Nam, l'histoire, la terre, les
hommes*, Paris 1987, 97ff.
Tran Tam Tinh, *Dieu et César*, 1978.
L. Cadieu, *Croyances et pratiques religieuses des Vietnamiens*, Saigon 1957–58.
Nguyen Hong, *Histoire de l'evangélisation au Viet Nam*, Viet Nam 1959.
Histoire de l'Eglise Catholique, Viet Nam 1972.

Being a Christian in Japan

Peter Nemeshegyi

More than 120 million people live on the four large and countless small islands which make up the territory of Japan, comprising 371,801 square kilometres. Of these approximately a million are baptized Christians who acknowledge Jesus Christ as their Lord and Redeemer. A small drop in a large ocean. But this small flock of Christ has a unique history and a great task.

A church of martyrs

The history of Christianity in Japan begins on 15 August 1549, when St Francis Xavier and two other Jesuits landed in the port of Kagoshima from the small boat of a Chinese merchant. They were the first Christian missionaries. Although it was outside the sphere of the colonial rule of Spain and Portugal, despite their defective knowledge of the language and their ignorance of Japanese social and religious conditions, the activity of these missionaries had amazing success. When Francis Xavier left the country in 1551 to prepare for his missionary journey to China – he died at its gates – there were several hundred baptized Christians in Japan and the doors had been opened to the evangelization of the country. First Jesuits and then also Dominicans, Franciscans and Augustinians of different nations came to Japan. Thanks to their selfless proclamation of the faith, by around 1580 their number had grown to an estimated 150,000, and by 1614 to 400,000. The newly converted included some who hoped that the acceptance of Christianity would bring them advantages in the mercantile trade with the Portuguese which was just beginning, but for most, acceptance of Christian faith was the consequence of an authentic conversion to God, the loving Father, and to Jesus Christ, the Redeemer who died for us.

Proof of the authenticity of these conversions can be seen in the heroic steadfastness of many Christians during the three-hundred-year-long persecution of Christians, begun by Shogun Toyotomi Hideyoshi[1] in 1587, intensified by his successor Tokugawa Ieyasu, and continued with unprecedented cruelty until 1873. Christianity was prohibited on pain of death, and the whole population was forced each year to trample on pictures of Christ and Mary to show that they were not Christians (many of these reliefs, stamped flat, are now in museums); all the ports of the land were barred to the outside world; many thousands of Christians who could not be persuaded to deny their faith even under the most excruciating torture were executed with the utmost cruelty; and all priests were either banished or suffered martyr deaths.

Nevertheless, more than 15,000 Christians, most of them simple fishermen or peasants, continued to practise their faith in secret, baptized their children and hoped for a better future. A French missionary, Bernard Petitjean (1829–84), who was given permission to be a pastor to foreigners living in Japan after the country had opened its ports as a result of pressure from the Western powers, discovered them in 1865. When their existence became known to the Japanese government, a last wave of cruel persecution descended on them, to which many fell victim, until finally in 1873 the ban on Christianity was lifted and freedom of religion was allowed in the 1889 constitution.

Before his death, one of those who were persecuted, Yūjirō by name (1855–70), a fifteen-year-old boy whom his tormentors forced to crouch naked in the open air for weeks on end, day and night in the winter cold, and whom they flogged every day, confided to his sister with whom he shared his prison: 'I was so freezing that I was ready to deny my faith. But then I saw a sparrow feeding its nestlings and protecting them from the wind with its wings. Then I understood that the heavenly Father also lovingly protects me, and I resolved to remain true to my faith no matter what people did to me.'

The followers of this steadfast Christian form a significant part of today's Japanese Catholics. Today they also include many priests and religious. In the last persecution, the inhabitants of the small village of Shitsu, near Nagasaki, were taken away and their fields were plundered; after they were allowed to return they lived in the utmost poverty. And yet two cardinals, Taguchi Yoshigoro (1902–1978) and Satowaki Asajirō (1904–), came from that village – something which is probably unique in church history.

Even after the promulgation of religious freedom, things were not easy for Christians in Japan. For three hundred years it had been drummed into the people with all the means of state propaganda that Christianity was an abhorrent religion and that Christians were traitors. Nevertheless, from the Meiji period on, great Christian figures appear in Japan. Before we turn to them, I would like first to sketch the spiritual situation of modern Japan in which they lived and worked as Christians.

The spiritual situation of modern Japan

The life of modern Japanese society is based on the following four elements: 1. the mystical religion transmitted through Buddhism; 2. Chinese culture and its Confucianism; 3. the original religion of the Japanese preserved in Shintoism; 4. Western science, technology, economics and art, Western legislation and education, and – since the end of the Second World War – democracy, freedom, equal rights and the welfare state. We need to consider these four elements briefly, since they are also very important for Christianity in Japan.

1. Buddhism came to Japan through China in its Mahayana form. This emphasizes the unity of all being in the primal nothingness of the Buddha nature. Human beings achieve their salvation in union with this original nature through experience of inner emptying or, as Amida Buddhism teaches, through trusting surrender to the Amida Buddha, who redeems all living beings by his great, merciful vow. Through the great Buddhist figures of the thirteenth century (Dōgen, Shinran, Nichiren), Buddhism in various forms spread throughout the population, and today Buddhist temples are still scattered all over the country, with bonzes offering their prayers and performing ceremonies within them.

However, the traditional sects of Buddhism have lost much of their force in modern Japan. One sign of this is that the bonzes in Japan, contrary to the teaching of Gautama Buddha, marry, and are mainly occupied in praying for the dead.

Still, the Buddhist mentality continues to have considerable influence on the soul of the Japanese. One sign of this is the more than 2,300 new religions which have come into being since 1867 and which have between twenty and thirty million Japanese adherents. The greatest of these religions follow the Lotus Sutra, and the others also transmit a good deal of Buddhist thought, though of a syncretistic kind, above all a conviction of the primal unity of all life in the cosmos. The great success of these new religions shows that the highly secularized Japanese society has a great religious need. Even among Japanese who do not belong to these new religions and have no particular personal religion, as is the case with many young people in the cities, there are many elements of the Buddhist mentality. Here are some of the most important of them:

(a) Awareness of the transitoriness of all that is earthly and the relaxed acceptance of this fact. The Japanese do not cling as tenaciously to the moment, or to personal life, as Westerners do.

(b) The Japanese are not egocentric. The 'I' is always felt to be embedded in a wider community: in the 'we' of the family, the business, the people.

(c) The Japanese feel bound up with all living being. They are very conscious of the different seasons of the year, they tend their gardens, they decorate their homes with seasonal flowers, and allude to changing nature in poems and letters.

(d) The Japanese feel the primal mystery in even the smallest things. They do not want to control this mystery through an objective view of it, but to fuse themselves with it by lifting the veil which divides the subject from the primal ground. The marvellous gardens of the Buddhist monasteries are not there for objective contemplation but are meant to communicate unity of experience with the one primal root of being.

2. As for Confucianism, while very few people nowadays call themselves Confucians, the main teachings of Confucius still prove to be a formative power in society. We can sum these teachings up in seven points:

(i) The aim of state rule is the general welfare of the people.

(ii) The prosperity of the people and of all other communities depends on the mutual benevolent collaboration of their members and is based on loyalty to the group and its leaders.

(iii) Leading positions in society are secured not by military rank or wealth but by a demonstration of proven knowledge.

(iv) Social life should be governed by a sense of duty and solidarity.

(v) Honour is due to those set in authority, to teachers and the old.

(vi) Courtesy is to be observed in social converse and in the ceremonies of religious and civil life.

(vii) It is not intellectual speculation but actions in accordance with the conscience that lead to true knowledge.

It is largely because of this Confucian ethos that Japanese society has developed into the second largest economic power in the world after its annihilating defeat in the Second World War, and even today functions relatively well.

Alongside the active virtues of Confucianism, however, another Chinese way of thinking is also alive in Japan: Taoism. In contrast to Kung-tse (Confucius), Lao-tse emphasizes not-doing, purposelessness, weakness, the feminine. The Japanese did not take over Taoism as a religion. Rather, as Gellért Béky writes in his fine book on Taoism, 'without Tao the delicate pictures of Chinese and Japanese painting, the almost supernatural refinements of pictorial art which express (or better suggest) something inexpressible with a minimum of expense and material, the unsurpassable mixture of colours in a kimono, the delightful glaze on Chinese porcelain, the hazy perfection of a Zen painting and yet more phenomena from the history of China and Japan are unthinkable'.[2]

3. Buddhism comes from India, and Confucianism and Taoism come from China; but even today Shinto is the living original religion of Japan. It has no dogmas and no doctrine of salvation. Its essence is the feast, where there is drumming, dancing and singing, and where people carry cultic objects around with rhythmic steps. Here the community celebrates its unity with the laughing primal harmony of all nature, unity with the dead ancestors, and unity with those now alive. Disputes and cares are forgotten in the cheerfulness: in trust, all feel their grounding in the universal life of the cosmos and its benevolent powers.

4. In the last one hundred and twenty years Japan, in which all these old traditions are alive, with an amazing capacity for learning has developed into the most modern society in the world. Its technology has overtaken that of the West, standards of living have risen considerably, democratic institutions are functioning, security generally is the best in the world, contributions to development, etc., have grown enormously, medical treatment is first class and average life-expectancy is the highest in the world.

However, the shadow side of modern life is not lacking. Financial scandals involving politicians are increasing, the divorce rate is rising, pornography and sexual promiscuity are rife, the abortion rate is enormous, juvenile delinquency is on the increase, the stress of life is doing much psychological damage, large numbers of failures who have been made homeless and vagabond eke out their wretched existence on the periphery of society, and Japan's aggressive trade policy is leading to conflicts with the strong countries and is detrimental to the weak.

This is the scene in which a series of great Christian personalities has worked and is working. Let us meet some of them and hear what they say.

Christian personalities in modern Japan

When Japan opened its ports in 1853 under pressure from Western armed forces, Christian missionaries also entered the country and became very active after the lifting of the ban on Christianity. Catholic missionaries from the Paris Missionary Society not only cared for the Christians who had survived from the Xavier period but in a traditional way developed vigorous missionary activity all over the country. Their indefatigable zeal, and the schools, hospitals and leprosaries founded by the French religious orders, led to the formation of many small Christian communities, but on the whole their influence on society remained small.

During this period the Protestant missionaries, who mostly came from America and founded a number of universities as early as the 1870s, exercised considerable influence on the educated classes, especially on the young samurai, who had lost their position in society because of the abolition of the feudal system and were seeking a new basis for their life. One of these was Ebina Danjō (1856–1937),[3] who became convinced as a result of his studies of Confucius that the Heaven often mentioned by Kung-tse was a personal God. He got into contact with Christian missionaries and was baptized. For him, in true Confucian fashion, God was the Lord whom he had to serve with absolute faithfulness. Later he regarded God more and more as his Father, with whom he felt united as a child. However, his christology was a kind of 'proving christology': for him Christ was an extraordinary personality who had fully realized the father-child relationship with God.

Because of this kind of christology, Ebina was involved in a dispute with another extraordinarily gifted convert to Protestantism, Uemura Masahisa (1861–1925), who on the basis of an overwhelming conversion experience advocated a strictly orthodox, Calvinistic doctrine and devoted his enormous energy to the foundation of church communities and to a prophetic ministry of social justice and humanity. Many of the later leaders of Japanese Protestantism were his pupils.

Uchimura Kanzō (1861–1930) was another very different figure. He felt his encounter with the Christian God to be a happy liberation from the slavery of all gods, and wanted to combine love for Jesus with love for Japan, Confucian ethics with Christian morality. Finally he found peace for his soul in belief in redemption by the cross of Christ, but he thought the multiplicity of institutional Christian churches offensive. So he founded the 'no-church movement'. According to Uchimura, Jesus wanted to found a community which did not consist of offices and orders but was formed through faith in the love of Jesus the Christ. Uchimura felt that the institutions of the Western churches were artificial: the church of God should be simple and naive. So to the end of his life he remained a free evangelist. A large number of scientists, educationalists and theologians count themselves among his disciples and followers.

During the difficult war years a Christian social movement developed in Japanese Protestantism; its most significant thinker was Nakajima Shigeru (1880–1946). He hoped for a great human society, to be brought about through socialism. For him 'Christ' was another name for the body, a universal principle which had realized itself to a supreme degree in Jesus of Nazareth.

The great influence of the theology of Karl Barth on Japanese Protestant theology begins at the same time. Many Japanese Christians are converts who found their conversion experience in the abrupt Barthian repudiation of all non-Christian religions. However, Barthian theology did not favour the acceptance of the above-mentioned elements of traditional Japanese religion. A positive critical discussion with other religions began only in the post-war years.

During the war the military government of Japan regarded Christianity with great mistrust. On the orders of the government, all Protestant churches were combined into a Christian Church of Japan, and the refusal of some Christians to take part in the Shinto ceremonies prescribed by the government was punished as high treason. In this situation, in 1936 the Roman Propaganda congregation published an instruction in which it allowed Japanese Catholics to take part in the ceremonies of the state Shinto temple on the basis of a declaration by the Japanese government that these ceremonies were not religious occasions but were purely patriotic. Similarly, Catholics were allowed to take part in the religious ceremonies usual in Japan at funerals and weddings.[4] This instruction drew a line under the unhappy history of the prohibition of Chinese rites – a prohibition which was perhaps the greatest mistake in missionary history – but the fact that this took place in connection with Japan's militarism still causes Japanese Christians pangs of conscience even now. Especially in Protestant circles, the feeling that many Christians failed during the war is great, and although the post-war constitution has left the emperor a mere symbol of state without political power, these circles tenaciously attack the Tenno system.

Finally, during the war significant thinkers also appeared among Japanese Catholic Christians. Along with the most highly gifted and holiest priest Iwashita Sōichi (1889–1940), mention should be made above all of his pupil Yoshimitsu Yoshihiko (1904–45). A student of the famous imperial university of Tokyo, full of ambitious plans for the future, he had an experience which he was later fond of calling his 'Hortensius experience': like Augustine on reading Cicero's *Hortensius*, he made the great decision to devote his life exclusively to searching for truth and striving for virtue. First he became a Protestant, then a Catholic, and studied with Jacques Maritain. His return to Japan was followed by twelve years of the most intensive spiritual creation in the service of the eternal Logos and the church of Christ. He taught philosophy at the Sophia University founded by Jesuits in 1911, wrote books and articles, and philosophized with the utmost dedication until his early death. 'East and West are one,' he wrote on his sick-bed. 'The revelation of the supernatural truth of Christianity which corresponds to the common sharing of all toils and efforts of human nature, brings everything to unity and consummation.' With shining eyes he said in his last lecture: 'The true Christian is the victor in the universe, the victor in human life. The basic melody of the music of his soul must be a constant "Alleluia, Amen". My friends, let us praise the Risen Lord standing in the centre of the universe with faces uplifted to the heavenly church, still in the earthly church.'

Another theology born in the pains of wartime is the theology of the pain of God presented by the Protestant theologian Kitamori Kazō (1916–). God the Father loves the sinners whom he really cannot love and gives his only-begotten Son for them. To do this represents deep pain for God the Father. Men who are willing to bear great pain for love are witnesses to the pain of God. These thoughts of Kitamori's developed in 1946 did not find much response among theologians in Japan at the time because of his criticism of Barth. But they aroused considerable interest in the West, as they anticipated the theologies of the suffering God which appeared in the 1960s.

Since the 1970s, a strong, radical movement has formed, particularly among the Protestant Christians of the Christian Church of Japan, involved in political and social action. Here Jesus is depicted as a man who took the side of a people who were suffering and discriminated against, and in contrast to the ruling classes of his time longed for a society which was more in keeping with human dignity. Christians in this group are deeply committed to the disadvantaged in Japanese society and energetically support the movements of social protest in other Asian countries.

Another area vigorously researched in the post-war years was christology, in a critical discussion with Buddhism and especially with the philosophy of Nishida Kitarō (1870–1945), which had a Buddhist stamp. The christology of the Protestant theologian Takizawa Katsuma (1906–84) is part of this trend. He calls the primal fact 'Immanuel'. By that he means the primary contact of human beings with God. God is always with us. If a person 'awakens' to this primal fact, a secondary contact with God comes about: religious life. For Takizawa, Jesus is a man who made secondary contact with God so completely that he can become the criterion for everything human.

Similar notions, though developed in critical discussion of Takizawa, are developed by Yagi Seiichi (1932–). He was already a Protestant Christian when as the result of an experience of illumination of a Zen kind he had a direct experience in which – as he says – reality showed him how it was before being shaped by the ideal. For Yagi, his theology, developed on this basis, is the basis of a very vigorous dialogue with Buddhists. However, it leads to a relativization of Christianity.

A significant attempt at mediation between the Japanese spiritual tradition and Christianity, without relativizing the latter, can be found in the works of the Jesuit Kadowaki Kakichi (1926–). After intensive studies of technology, Christian philosophy and theology, Kadowaki devoted himself to Zen meditation under the guidance of a Zen master, during which he attained an enlightenment which his master recognized as authentic. In his book *Metaphysics of the Way*,[5] written out of a personal experience and inner compulsion, he explains and compares, from the perspective of a way, the thought-world of the great Japanese poet Bashō, the great Zen master Dōgen and Christianity. His exposition of Christianity based on the Gospel of John seeks to offer readers help in identifying with the way of 'Christ' with their whole personalities. In the beginning 'was' the divine being and the divine action which brings about the redemption of the world through the descent and ascent of the Logos. The paradox of the incarnation of God in Jesus is set in motion by the will of the Father for universal redemption. Corporeality plays a decisive role in all this: the disciples of Jesus are to hear the words of Jesus with their whole bodies and appropriate him. The pain of the Father when he 'abandons' his Son on the cross is the deepest of all pains. But in the resurrection Jesus draws all his disciples into 'hyper-loving community' with the Father.

Being a Japanese Christian

Here I must end my account of Japanese Christian thinkers, though many other names could have been mentioned. To sum up, we could discuss the main tasks of Christianity in Japan in the following points:

1. Christianity in Japan may not understand itself as a merely prophetic religion which exclusively confesses the 'wholly other', transcendent God. God who already dwells in every creature through creation, and the Holy Spirit of Christ, works in each individual at every moment of his or her life. The primal fact is 'God with us', who surrenders himself in humble, prodigal love. Only if Jesus is Son of God in the most real sense of the world can the cross of Jesus be understood as the place of the pain of God, where Father and Son, each in their own way, share in the pain of the world. The resurrection of Christ is the foundation for hope in the victorious, eternal success of the great cosmic life which we cannot describe, but only have intimations of and hope for.

2. Meister Eckhardt already remarked that 'two as one is love'. The

Christian theology of the East must be a theology of love and goodness. The transcendent God makes himself a living way in every individual and all of humankind, for whose universal salvation we may hope. Christ is God's irrevocable affirmation in the world, the 'Yes' of God 'who loves life' (Wisdom 11.26).

3. Christianity in Japan must address the inner religious depths of the human soul. It cannot run away in activism. Nor may it forget the unity of soul and body. Doing theology in Japan should be the treading of a way on which Christians walk with the commitment of their whole being in the discipleship of Christ. This is a journey the soul of which is prayer surrounded by the stillness of God.

4. The social and caritative commitment of Christians remains essential. But it must be based on a deep religious experience and take account of the values of Confucian ethics. However, these ethics as currently practised in Japan need correction. The communities in Japan which function well within groups are mostly closed communities which are indifferent, competitive or hostile to outsiders. An extension of the ethical attitude to all of humankind is necessary. It was already envisaged by Kung-tse, but finds its ultimate foundation in faith in the Father of all human beings and in Christ who died and rose again for all. Moreover traditional morality in Japan has largely lost its original metaphysical and religious foundation. It needs a new foundation which can best be offered by belief in the trinitarian God of creation.

5. In the face of exaggerated organization and purposefulness, Christianity in Japan should speak more of the weakness, purposelessness and lavish generosity of Christian love. Jesus was criticized by his kinsfolk as not being purposeful (John 7.3–4), and St Bernard of Clairvaux says of love: 'I love because I love. Love is the ground of love' (*In Cant*. 83.4). Japan has produced a series of Protestant amd especially Catholic writers (Endō Shūsaku, Miura Ayako, Ogawa Kunio, Sono Ayako, Inukai Michiko, Tanaka Sumie and many others) whose novels, narratives and reports have been read by millions of Japanese. The favourite theme of these writers is Jesus disarmed by love itself, who supports weak, trembling, stumbling men and women to the end. Both these writers and the good reputation of Christian schools and charitable institutions have contributed a good deal to the positive assessment of the history of Japanese Christianity today and the high esteem in which Christianity is held.

6. The primal harmony intimated in the Shinto Festival is a reality; it is the loving community of the triune God. All comes from him and strives to return to him, until he becomes 'all in all' (II Cor. 15.28). This faith gives the Christian a deep optimism.

7. The ideals of human rights, equality in law, the welfare state, internationalism and so on, which ultimately come from Christianity, were taken over by the Japanese without their Christian roots. So they have no foundation. This foundation can and should be offered by Christianity. What is also lacking is the stimulus for realizing these ideals which stems from the faith that Jesus died out of love for us and all human beings, and that thanks to his resurrection love abides for ever. This stimulus can and should provide a christology which in Japan proves by word and deed that God is good.

Translated by John Bowden

Notes

1. In this article the Japanese family names are given first, as is the custom in Japan. The transcription follows Hepburn's system.
2. Gellért Béky, *Die Welt des Tao*, Freiburg and Munich 1972, 188.
3. For a detailed account of Japanese theology see A. Dohi, T. Sato, S. Yagi and M. Odagaki, *Theologiegeschichte der Dritten Welt, Japan*, Munich 1991.
4. *Acta Apostolicae Sedis* 28, 1936, 406–9.
5. Kadowaki Kichi, *Michi no keijiōgaku, Bashō, Dōgen, Iseu*, Tokyo 1990.

The Christian Workers' Fellowship of Sri Lanka

Tissa Balasuriya

The Christian Workers' Fellowship is one of the earliest and foremost church-related non-governmental organizations in Sri Lanka. The movement was begun by a group of Christian workers in 1958, in part due to the influence of the social eruption of the people of Sri Lanka, especially among the Sinhala masses at the general elections of April 1956, six years after Independence in February 1948. The 1956 political change manifested to the whole country the need of radical social changes to meet the aspirations of the majority of the people, especially the Sinhala and Buddhists. It was a protest against the privileges enjoyed by the English-speaking elite, in wealth, incomes, education, employment and social life.

It also revealed to the discerning Christians how estranged they were from the majority who were poor and mainly Buddhist and Hindu. This was the period when a resurgent Buddhist leadership was demanding the nationalization of the schools which were run by denominational bodies, principally Christians. When Sri Lanka became independent, the Christians, benefitting from colonial rule, were a privileged minority, with advantages as a result of their better opportunities for education.

At the middle of this century the Christian churches in Ceylon, as the island was called then, were largely insensitive to their social responsibilities. The more enlightened among them, such as Fr Peter Pillai, Canon Ekanayake and Dr C. J. C. de Silva, were in favour of social reforms within the framework of capitalism. They were afraid of Communism and thought the Marxist parties such as the Lanka Sama Samaja Party and the Communist Party were the principal threat to the country and to the churches, whose progress was the main goal of their mission. In the general elections of this period the Catholic church authorities enjoined on their members to vote for the right-wing parties and not for Marxists or their allies, who favoured the nationalization of the schools.

The churches locally and globally were far from evolving a theology of dialogue with the other religions. The schools were nationalized in 1960–61 largely through the refusal of the Christians, especially Catholics, to allow other religions to be taught in their schools to students of those religions. The prevalent Christian theology was that Christianity is the only true religion, and others are false. The church leadership was almost wholly exercised by the clergy or by a lay elite who had the approbation of the bishops and clergy. The church apostolate among the workers, if it went beyond the traditional pastoral functions of the clergy, was of a paternalist nature. A few organizations, such as the Social Justice Movement, the Young Christian Workers and the Catholic Workers' Movement, were more socially conscious.

The Christian Workers' Fellowship (CWF) was born in Colombo city in 1958 as an informal group of predominantly English-speaking white-collar Christian workers. Vijaya Vidyasagara, a unionist and lawyer, later a public servant in the Department of Inland Revenue, was one of the principal initiators, ideologues, organizers and liturgists of the movement, and still remains active. Among the other pioneers were Earle Keegel, Jeffrey Abeysekera, Audrey Rebera, Ainsley Samarajiwa, F. R. Rasiah and I. P. C. Mendis. Since they were motivated by religion committed to social change and involved in political action, they had to grapple with the problems of religion and Maraxism as well as inter-religious relations.

Among the chief characteristics of the movement are its:
  (i) lay character, in leadership, theology and liturgy;
 (ii) non-denominational nature, functioning outside the institutional church structures (but recognized by the churches);
(iii) openness to all the churches and inter-communion among them;
 (iv) commitment to inter-religious dialogue, action and worship;
  (v) Socialist left orientation in thinking and political action.

The first three of these considerations deal with intra-church and inter-church relations. The lay leaders of the CWF have the advantage of being well versed in the theology and liturgy of the churches as well as the Marxist thinking and practice in the country. Some of them were members of the left-political parties and were placed in a tricky situation as convinced Christians who found meaning in the kernel of the gospel message of Jesus Christ. But they found most members of the church leadership unsympathetic to their thinking and left-orientation or even commitment to political issues as a Christian group. On the other hand, the right-wing political parties had no satisfactory solution to the problems of the workers, or for the liberation of the country from local and foreign capitalism.

They wanted to participate in the worship of the church, but found the traditional liturgical services formalistic and divorced from both the problems of the workers and from the religions and culture of the majority of the Sri Lankan people. For such reasons also these workers formed their own movement, without seeking or expecting a church mandate. They had to evolve their own theology and liturgy in the context of the religious, social and culture context of Sri Lanka.

The CWF is one of the first experiences of a non-denominational Christian movement. Today we know of the 'post-denominational' church formed by the different Protestant churches in China. In 1958 in Sri Lanka, it was a truly pioneering effort to bring together Christian workers of all the denominations, including the Catholics. The CWF was begun before good Pope John XXIII's reforms (1958–1963), the Second Vatican Council (1962–1965), and the changes being pioneered by the World Council of Churches reached Sri Lanka.

The lay movement had among its membership bishops Lakshman Wickremasinghe, Anglican, and Leo Nanayakkara OSB, Catholic, the two forward-looking bishops of the period 1960–1984. Priest-theologians Aloysius Pieris, SJ, Lynn de Silva, Methodist, and Kenneth Fernando (elected Anglican Bishop of Colombo in May 1992), and several other clergy were active supporters of the movement. The CWF was able to bring together clergy of the churches even when the churches themselves were rather far from each other. From an early stage they fostered inter-communion among the Christians of all denominations. The clergy of all the churches participated actively in the liturgies developed by the CWF, especially the Workers' Mass. This naturally involved a challenge to the traditional orthodoxy of each church.

Theology of the church

The crisis of confidence in the church evoked different responses in this period. Some priests and religious in the Catholic church found it not possible to exercise a meaningful ministry within the then rigid structures of the church and they returned to the lay state, giving up the struggle within their clerical or religious positions. Some left the priesthood or religious congregations, as they wanted to change their life-style and enter the married state. Some others migrated as priests and/or religious to other countries where their thinking was more readily accepted.

Some others remained in Sri Lanka, though discontented with the church's institutional structures, and tried to evolve new ways of Christian presence and witness, without leaving the church or ministry or being restricted to its limited orientations. The CWF contributed towards bringing them together and helped to articulate a theology more in keeping with our Sri Lankan heritage of Buddhism, Hinduism and Islam. The CWF sought an expression of their faith in Jesus Christ that could inspire them to social commitment as well as communion with other religions.

Recalling the ancient Christian tradition, they saw the meaning of the church in a broader sense than was then common in the churches.

> Christianity is not just 'pie in the sky' as some folks imagine. It has very much to do with the living of our daily lives here and now. Nor is Christianity merely an individualistic religion, intensely personal but with little or nothing to say about social and secular matters. On the contrary, to a Christian, *the claim of Christ is a total claim*. It is valid over the whole life, whether public or private, spiritual or material, religious or secular. The Redeemer of the soul is also the Saviour of the Body: the Lord of the Church is also the Lord of the world . . . And all men are brothers because they have a common Father who made them in His own image and in Christ they have a common Brother who shared their life and work and ultimately died that their total life may be more abundant.

These words come from *The Christian Worker and the Trade Union*, the first document of the CWF, issued in November 1958, some months after the group began to form itself.

The twelve-page pamphlet exhorts the workers to take part in trade-union activities and where necessary in political life as a necessary consequence of discipleship of Christ. At this stage the quotations are mainly from the Old and New Testaments and the Fathers of the church, taken from the writings of British thinkers. The references to the early Fathers of the Church are noteworthy from the earliest CWF document. Thus they quote St Clement of Alexandria (c. 210):

> All things are common and not for the rich to appropriate an undue share. The expression, therefore, 'I possess and possess it in abundance, why should I not enjoy', is suitable neither to man nor to society . . . God has given us the liberty of use, but only so far as necessary, and He has determined that the use should be common (*Paed 2:13*, in *The Christian Worker and the Trade Union*, 8).

They also quote St Basil (c. 379), St John Chrysostom (c. 407), the medieval John Ball of Kent (1381, priest and leader of a peasant uprising in

England), Jerrard Winstanley (seventeenth-century leader of the Diggers Movement in England), John Malcolm Ludlow (1821–1911, a pioneer of the Christian Socialist Movement in England) and others. The last passage is from Frederick Engels' Introduction to Karl Marx's *The Class Struggles in France*, 6 March 1895. Camilo Torres is quoted in the 1976 revised reprint.

Thus the inspiration of the beginnings was an indigenous reflection on the local situation motivated by the left-Christian thinking available in English at the time. This was prior to subsequent developments in ecumenical and liberation theologies of the 1960s and 1970s.

This vision was later developed more clearly in its implications in their pamphlet *For a* Real *Sri Lankan Church* (Colombo 1984). It begins with a reflection on the mystery of the divine.

> *The whole of humanity (not* just Christians) is the family and mystical body of God: the Church exists only as an outward sign and symbol of that truth and as an effective means for its realization. Thus the Church does not exist for herself but to serve human beings in building 'the kingdom' or 'righteous rule' of God among people, so that they all may truly live in brotherhood (*sic*), justice and peace as God's family. In short, the Church is the Sacrament of the Kingdom (1–2).

From these basic principles they developed further applications in actual church and social life. The church

> is said to exist from the beginning of the human race, and since the foundation of the world (Ephesians 1.4). So if the Church was preexisting, she was existing then in all the saints who lived since the beginning of time, whatever their religious beliefs or credal affirmations.

The church in a wider sense would thus be coterminous with all persons who did the will of God regardless of their religious professions (Matthew 7.21; Acts 10.34–35; Matthew 25). The CWF thinking witnessed to the Holy Spirit as present to the whole of humanity (Romans 15.21; Isaiah 52.15).

> Christ is the expectation of the peoples (Genesis 49.10). His spirit is at work among non-believers (Romans 15.21; Isaiah 52.15) and is even found by those who do not seek him (*sic*) (Romans 10.20; Acts 17.23)) . . . The Christian Faith believes that God who has spoken through the prophets and sages of old – through the Buddhas and rishis

– has finally sent His living word in Christ to demonstrate the dynamic truth that underlies all justice and all dharmas.

From this the CWF argued that in God's universal providence

then there must necessarily be some link between the traditional religions of Asia and the religion of His Son Jesus. There is thus a need to go beyond religious labels to discern the fruits of God's Spirit, which has been and is now at work in the world, in 'non-Christian' religions and in secular ideologies of liberation. This must also lead us to a recognition of our traditional Asian faiths such as Hinduism and Buddhism as genuine vehicles of salvation given by God in their respective contexts (2–3).

The theology of the 'Logos' is understood in the wider sense of Christ as the active saving presence of God in all creation in and through their religio-cultural realities. This includes a sacramental theology that en-globes the other religions as sacraments. We can apply to them the traditional Christian definition of a sacrament as 'the outward sign of inward grace'.

Christ is the Word or expression of God, the Logos, the Dharma and the Dynamic of history, who provides all human beings coming into existence with the means of salvation, the path of liberation in their own religio-cultural contexts . . . It is through the sacraments of Buddhism and Hinduism, through the message of morality and the self-giving life, that such salvation is normally transmitted and received . . .

It is only when, through the working of Christ, the spiritual treasures found in these ancient religious streams and Christianity merge in a single river, that we will discover the face of a truly Asian Christ (15).

The CWF develops a christology by taking the basic assertions of the scriptures and giving them meaning in our context, without going into the imaginative and endless debates about the dogmatic definitions of the churches.

In our Buddhist-Hindu tradition, Dharma is essentially that which gives meaning and holds all life together and which leads the world from darkness to light, from death to immortality. This can only be considered in terms of the great struggle for liberation ('vimukthi') of all beings. Dharma is basically identified with justice and righteousness and the fight against evil in all its forms. 'Christ' is the Judeo-Christian account ('myth') of this divine disclosure in the events of history (Exodus; 1 Corinthians 10.1–4).

From its commencement the CWF was open to the other religions while having a Christian and socialist outlook. From the Bible itself they deduce the presence of the Spirit in other religious traditions.

> Although the Bible unfurls the story of 'Dharmic' action in Jewish history, it recognizes that the scope of the Dharma's liberating action goes far beyond the confines of Jewish and Christian history (Amos 9.7; Isaiah 19.24–25; Micah 4.1–5; Romans 8.18–24). Unfortunately this profound insight has been by and large lost sight of by the Semitic-European religious traditions and their missionary endeavour. The true Asian Church in formation must therefore allow itself to be transfigured through and through until it shows forth the unparalleled beauty of the Dharma in its fullness (16).

The Christian sacraments are interpreted in relation to this wider perspective and the actual living of the moral life in the day-to-day situations of society. Thus baptism is a commitment to foster the reign of righteousness and to combat the forces of evil of which Mammon is a principal manifestation in our times.

They were inspired by scientific social analysis, the demand of social justice and Marxist thought. Over the years they worked out the synthesis of these different elements through their understanding of the mystery of Christ in its broadest significance. Drawing from the Orthodox tradition of Sts Basil and John Chrysostom the CWF endeavoured to live the

> Sacrament of the Brother which is basically the Sacrament of the Poor. It is the Sacrament of the Poor because in the presence of the brother, who is on our side, we see the mystery of the presence of Christ challenging us to open our heart and to share in solidarity the struggle for the satisfaction of the human needs of the brother (Matthew 25.31–46) and so proceed towards transforming all social conditions that prevent and obstruct the satisfaction of such needs (4).

This was the Christian motivation of the social concern and commitment of the CWF. While the poor are the principal agents of their liberation and a call to the others to respond to the demands of righteousness, the rich too have to liberate themselves from selfishness, and being oppressors. Their liberation or 'vimukthi' is also in overcoming acquisitiveness and attachment to wealth to the disadvantage of others.

The CWF liturgy

The traditional Christian liturgy has been and still constitutes a problem for the more socially conscious Christians. This is because this worship has been clerically dominated, denominationally exclusive, largely divorced from liberative action in society and with little relevance to the cultural and spiritual traditions of the Sri Lankan people. There has been little readiness in the mainline churches to be seriously open to these dimensions despite their rhetoric. On the other hand the charismatic, Pentecostal and fundamentalist groups provide for much lay participation but some of them are not quite concerned with the social issues, and have strong reservations concerning the communion with other religions.

The CWF has rendered a signal contribution to the liturgical life of the Christians in the country by developing forms of worship that endeavour to meet these needs of inter-Christian communion, social relevance, lay particpation or initiative and inter-religious relations. In this their theology of an open and socially responsible christology has enabled them to develop the spirituality in all these dimensions.

The common life of the CWF is characterized by the regular celebration of the Workers' Mass at which the presence of persons of other faiths and persuasions is a natural and welcome feature. The Workers' Mass, which has been drawn up by lay CWF members, brings out clearly the vision of the classless society and life as it should be lived in the freedom of Jesus, 'the Man for others'. It thus provides a dynamic for social action to persons of all persuasions. It has many Sinhala and Hindu-Buddhist elements such as the silence, the chants, the drums, the conch shell, the use of water, lights, fire, incense, the veneration of the sacrament by profound bowing, and the Hindu sense of worship of the Transcendent: Om Shanti Shanti Shanti. The workers' radical orientations are expressed by invoking the memory of the great leaders of active non-violence such as Mahatma Gandhi and Martin Luther King, and of the revolutionary processes such as Marx and Engels, Camilo Torres, Che Guevara. The Red Flag and instruments of work are offered at the altar with bread and wine and carried away at the end of the service to the accompaniment of the Sri Lankan equivalent of the Internationale, thus linking the Mass to the mass struggles.

The CWF understanding of the eucharist as sharing in the sacrifice and love of Christ inspires its openness to inter-communion with all persons of goodwill who opt for the values of the reign of righteousness preached by Jesus. It is not bound by the rigidities of the official church denominations. On the other hand it insists on the social significance of the eucharist, so that

it becomes impossible for a conscious Christian, who knows what the

Holy Communion means, not to be involved in the struggle for human liberation, impossible for an earnest communicant not to be an earnest politician.

The CWF has evolved other forms of liturgy such as the Holy Week services linked to their Bible studies, the Fellowship Meal (Agape), rites for Baptism, weddings, funerals, repentance and healing, and meditation such as Maithri Bhavana (meditation on compassion). It has been fostering an architecture and church decoration that expresses the inter-religious dimension of our society and God's universal presence in humanity.

The truly Asian church is yet to be. It will have to be born out of the merging of our spiritual traditions.

What the Church as the Body of Christ will look like then can only be a matter of conjecture. But we would do well to distinguish the present image of the Christian Church from the Asian Church that is yet to be! (13).

Socio-political commitment and trade-union work

The principal activity of the CWF is in the service of the workers by helping in their ongoing education, their organization and joining in their struggles. It has published valuable social studies reflecting on the recent history of the country. Its major work, *Social Change in Ceylon*, published as a pamphlet in 1968, soon became popular in both academic and working-class circles.

The CWF has helped to bring Christians to take a keen interest in the cause of the workers, insisting on the oneness of the human and the divine or spiritual. At the same time the workers of all persuasions have been able to see the Christian concern for the common cause of liberation of the people. Throughout the country's problems of the past few decades, the CWF has played a positive and constructive role with its links with the working classes and its membership that cuts across racial and religious differences.

As a non-denominational lay movement outside the institutional structures, the CWF had the necessary freedom and flexibility for real involvement and identification with the worker's movement. The Fellowship had its trials and differences of opinion on matters of ideology as well as of a personal nature. However, during thirty five years it has been able to resolve its problems by consensus, providing for unity in diversity with its collective form of leadership.

The CWF has spread from the base of the industrial workers in Colombo to the rest of the country: the plantation workers, free-trade-zone workers and farmers. Its 'Gami Seva Sevana' in Galaha near Kandy is a project for the promotion of organic farming. It has helped to form farmers' co-operatives to counteract the big multinationals that are taking over the food-processing, distribution and even production in the country. The CWF units encourage community living in different forms along with the sharing of religious experiences and social commitment.

With its branches in all the provinces of the country, the CWF has helped actively in trying to find a just and peaceful solution to the ethnic conflict that has ravaged Sri Lanka during the past decade. It has been able to keep contact with members in all parts of the country during our civil war that has divided many other groups on ethnic lines. It has presented a political option for a united Sri Lanka based on genuine devolution to the provinces. In the process the CWF organizer in Kantale was killed in April 1989 for trying to create a 'peace zone' in a racially sensitive area. During the past decade, all these activities have been fraught with grave danger to life because of many armed groups, legal and illegal, operating in the country and taking the law into their own hands.

The CWF quarterly publication *The Christian Worker* is one of the best journals in the country. Its 'yellow pages' give a very informative and critical analysis of events and issues in the country and the world. It is read by the leadership of all the main political parties, especially of the left.

Impact and significance

Begun by an English speaking group in Colombo, the CWF now works throughout the country mainly in Sinhala and Tamil. The different combinations of orientations and activities make it a pioneer in a number of fields: lay leadership, Christian theology, meaningful liturgy, Christian art and liturgical music, inter-religious relations, Christian-Marxist dialogue, social and political commitment inspired by religion, and religions purified by social engagement. In all these dimensions it has been a pathfinder and trailblazer.

Appendix: Extract from the Statement of the Consultation on African and Asian Spirituality, Colombo, 18–25 June 1992

(Tissa Balasuriya)

II. AFRICAN AND ASIAN SPIRITUALITY

New Awareness

A horizon of meaning

29. In this hour of history, in a situation such as has been described above, we need a new horizon of meaning – a fresh prioritizing of values, and a human, humane, style of living and sharing maize and rice and water, and the earth and the sky. We need a spirituality based on the dignity of every person, on our social and cosmic interdependence, and life's rootedness in matter. We need a spirituality of sustained struggle for freedom and justice, a spirituality of unrelenting resistance to domination and every sort of dictation emanating from the centres and institutions of accumulated wealth and power. *A spirituality that will train us to fight in defence of our right to shape our future, to define our goals and to tread the path we choose instead of letting our minds be colonized, our lands and their resources mortgaged, and our destiny hijacked by the creators of world poverty and traders in death.* Erstwhile colonizers, present exploiters and merchants of death and their local allies cannot provide models and definitions of the human nor of authentic human development. We have to define these basic realities for ourselves. Ours will be a spirituality *of the power of powerlessness, of the power of truth and love and freedom, a spirituality of the unyielding*

cross and its clean affirmations. It will be a spirituality of dissent and defiance, like a lighted lamp in the dark night.

Africa, Asia and the Bible

30. There is deep affinity between the traditional spirituality of Africa and Asia and the further spiritual growth we now aspire to; and between these and the spirituality of the Bible. All of them hinge on and spring from oppressed communities' experience of nature and history; their experience of the earth's beauty and bounty, of painful events, of suffering, struggles and hopes. African and Asian spirituality or religiousness, no less than that of the Bible, is concerned for life-giving blessings, not only in the after-life, but also within this world and within present history. It is a spirituality that thinks and acts and feels history and the cosmos, time and space; it is focussed on the unfolding of life on the stage of History on the face of this earth – of life with its story of joys and frustrations, rice and hunger, oppressions and liberations. This spirituality is global and cosmic in that it understands salvation in terms of life-giving blessings for humanity individually and collectively, envisioning all this to happen in a new world and a new history. By life-giving blessings we mean food, rain, shelter, land, human rights and dignity, freedom, justice, forgiveness of sin, the Spirit in people's hearts – in short, the fullness of life. It is cosmic because its desire is to see justice done to the victims of the system, to the 'orphan, widow, refugee, poor' who are paradigms of the oppressed and the marginalized; and this desire amounts to a major passion. It is cosmic also in the sense that its salvific concern embraces Nature, that is, the earth, the air, the trees and seas and birds.

Nature

31. Biblical religiousness has a special link with nature and the earth: not only because it thrived for the most part in an agricultural milieu; not only because it understands human salvation in terms of being blessed with 'grain, wine, oil, the young of the flock and the herd, the spirit within human hearts' and the coming of a 'new heaven and a new earth' (Jer. 31.12; Ex. 36.26–30; Isa. 65.17–25; Rev. 21.1–5); not only because nature was frequently on their lips when the biblical people prayed (cf. Ps.65, etc.); not only because Jesus was evidently close to the earth, the lilies of the field and the birds of the air.

32. But most especially because it sees the *earth and nature itself*, not only humanity, *as a focus of God's salvific concern*. We sense this in the

way the creation story is crafted, five days being dedicated to the earth, light, waters, plants, trees, birds, cattle, and they were all good (Gen. 1.1–25); the earth is a beautiful garden (Gen. 2.8–9). The second creation is launched with a covenant not only with Noah but also with 'every living creature – the birds, the livestock, and all the wild animals . . . every living creature on earth' (Gen. 9.9ff.).

33. We see this in a special way in the biblical vision of future salvation: 'And on that day I will make a covenant with the beasts of the field, the birds of the air, and the creeping things of the ground' (Hos. 2.18–20). Or again, 'The wolf shall dwell with the lamb . . .' (cf. Isa. 11.1–9). Ultimate salvation is expressed by Paul in terms representative of Semitic thinking: *'Creation waits with eager longing . . . to be set free from its bondage to decay and obtain the glorious liberty of the children of God . . . Creation has been groaning in travail . . . '* (Rom. 8.19–23). Thus salvation history which began with the creation of heaven and earth (Gen. 1.1) will be consummated in the crafting of a new heaven and a new earth (Rev. 21.1–5). Ephesians sees the unity and summation of all things, not just humanity, in Christ (Eph. 1.9–10). Paul sees that when all things are subject to Jesus, 'God will be all in all' (I Cor. 15.28) – a vision of things which links us closely to the Oneness of All of the great religions of the East.

Conversion

34. We must therefore repent of our ruthless dominance over nature. The consequences of such dominance are devastating; they have begun to make themselves felt with a vengeance. Our attempts to be dominators of the universe instead of being its stewards and friends have distorted and destroyed our relationship with nature. Possessiveness and greed have replaced the caring, brotherly-sisterly bond that ought to have held us and the earth together. The resultant warped relations manifest themselves in capitalism and patriarchy. These exploit and debase both earth and woman, the mysterious source and base of life and future's promise. The ecological crisis and women's protests and the cry of the dispossessed are now forcing us to acknowledge the futility of attempts to coerce nature into submission with the wizardry and abstractions of our science and technology. They are forcing us to go back to our cosmic and social roots in order to recoup our radical earthiness and to re-establish our symbiotic relationship with the rest of creation. They are inviting us, prodigal sons and daughters of the cosmos, to repent of our self-inflicted brokenness and our class, race and sexist divisions; and to find healing and communion in

holistic harmonious relationships with nature and women and men. Instead of seeking fulfilment in domination and power, we are called to a life of interdependence within the cosmic Web of Life; and to a spirituality that will ground us firmly within the cosmic reality and the network of human fellowship; and will underscore the complementarity and equality of all persons, groups and cultures without discriminations and privileges based on sexist, racist or colour prejudices, or on one's capacity for violence. It is a spirituality that seeks to realize itself in mutual acceptance and understanding of one another, and in the production and sustenance of life beyond all competitive exploitation of nature or people.

35. African and Asian spirituality is also *ecologically integrated*. The very survival and progress of humankind is intrinsically and inseparably linked to our willingness and ability to co-exist with nature. Besides providing basic survival resources for the sustenance of life, nature also presents us with myriad sounds and sights of indescribable beauty to inspire and uplift the human spirit and imagination. This spirituality creates in us a renewed sense of wonder and appreciation of the unparalleled beauty and rhythm of nature and see ourselves as an integral part of the cosmos.

Justice

36. African and Asian spirituality emphasizes the truth which the Bible, too, underscores, that the earth and its resources are not for the benefit of a few persons, nor for the benefit of one – our – generation alone. They are for the good of the whole humankind, including those yet to be born. The spirituality we are concentrating on points to a life of sharing in simplicity and non-acquisitive sobriety. It promotes 'being more' in shared fellowship rather than 'having more' in individualist accumulation. This new life is made possible by community control of the common material basis of life and by responsible use of the earth's resources for the good of the whole human family.

37. The spirituality in question therefore educates us to the contemplation of God's justice-love enshrined and disclosed in birds and flowers and all creation. It urges us to struggle relentlessly for the victory of God's justice in all human transactions and for its universal reign on our earth (Matt. 5.3–11; 6.25–33; 25.31–46). A passion for the justice of God which provides every creature with all that it needs in order to be, to act and to become complete, will lead us to eschew greed and individualism, to analyse the cause of dehumanizing inequalities, and to join the struggles of

the poor and the oppressed for their liberation rather than salving one's conscience by resorting to palliatives and 'charities'.

38. Many indigenous peoples continue to draw energy and inspiration from their cosmic religiousness in their struggles and protests against anti-cosmic/anti-human forces of capitalism and imperialism. Unlike religiosities that promote 'other-worldliness' which prevents the emergence of a socially engaged spirituality and praxis, African-Asian-biblical spirituality promotes a 'this-worldliness' and commitment to history and the earth without degrading material things through atheistic contempt or idolatrous greed. This spirituality involves us in action for integral human rights, including woman's rights over her body and her sexuality. It has planetary dimensions calling for a sharing of land and its resources among all peoples. That entails a call for justice in population-distribution over the earth's surface, correcting the present land-population ratio which came to be in the wake of Columbus and Vasco da Gama and Magellan and Cortes and Europe's colonial expansion. Our spirituality is thus a multi-faceted invitation for all to participate in envisioning and realizing a new life which claims wholeness for the earth and the entire cosmos.

39. Our spirituality is rooted in and centred on our life and life's experiences. So too is the religiousness of the Bible. The Bible is about history: history is its basic and over-arching 'theme'. It is concerned with the history for the story of the Israelite people (Gen. 12–50, Exodus to Deuteronomy, I Samuel to II Kings, Nehemiah and Ezra, the prophetic books are all critical comments on Israelite history).

40. It will be helpful to meditate on the credal statements (e.g. Deut. 26.5–10) of the Israelite religion. It celebrates, not metaphysical dogmas, but *events in the religio-political history of Israel*: the call and the migrations, the peace and prosperity in Egypt under Joseph, the liberation, the possession of the land.

41. Israelite faith sees these events as Yahweh's deeds in history. Thus we note that the biblical God who certainly exhibits 'metacosmic' characteristics (the God 'up there in heaven', Isa. 6.1–8; Ps. 33.13–14; Matt. 5.9), is understood as also very much 'incarnate' in historical events.

42. It is concerned with the theological story of *humankind and of the world* (Gen. 1–11; Isa. 40–66, Jewish Apocalyptic writings, Romans, Ephesians, Revelation, the Kingdom message of Jesus).

43. This story stretches *from the creation of heaven and earth in the beginning* (Gen. 1–3) *to the coming of the new heaven and new earth at the end of this present history* (see Rev. 21).

44. And the centre of this history is Jesus Christ, his works, his death and resurrection and his 'coming again' in glory.

Salvation as life-giving blessings

45. In the *Hebrew Scriptures* (the Old Testament) *future salvation* is envisioned as God's Spirit outpoured, abundance of the fields, justice and right, peace (as the fruit of justice) and security and similar blessings. Isaiah provides an example:

46. ' . . . The Spirit is poured upon us from on high, and the wilderness becomes a fruitful field, and the fruitful field is deemed a forest.
Then justice will dwell in the wilderness, and righteousness abide in the fruitful field.
And the effect of righteousness will be peace, and the result of righteousness, quietness and trust for ever.
My people will abide in a peaceful habitation, in secure dwellings, and in quiet resting places.
Happy are you who sow beside all waters, who let the feet of the ox and the ass range free' (Isa. 32.15–20).

47. *Salvation in the present* consists in the salvific blessings of land, rains, abundant harvest, bread, security, peace, progeny, covenant, God with the people, liberation from slavery (see Lev. 26.2–13).

48. *In the Christian Scriptures* (the New Testament), *future salvation* consists in a new creation or a new world in which justice is at home. Thus, 'according to God's promise, we wait for new heavens and new earth where justice dwells' (II Peter 3.13). The Book of Revelation describes this new world as a place where a new humanity is God's covenanted people and among whom God dwells, where tears are wiped away, and death and mourning and pain are no more, where all things are made new (Rev. 21.1–5). The Beatitudes portray this salvation, both present and future, as a new world and a new history where the life-blessings are divine sonship and daughtership, direct experience of God, experience of God's compassion, possession of the earth, rice/bread, justice and liberation for the poor (Matt. 5.2–10; Luke 6.20–21).

49. *Salvation in the present* consists in health to the sick, life to the dead and good news (of justice and liberation) to the poor and oppressed – all different dimensions of life.

50. And Jesus answered them, 'Go and tell John what you hear and see: the blind receive their sight and the lame walk, lepers are cleansed and the deaf hear, and the dead are raised up, and the poor (*'anawim* = the oppressed poor) have good news preached to them.' (see Matt. 11.2–5).

51. *Justice*, particularly what we call today 'social justice', is more central in the biblical religion and spirituality than we might expect, particularly in the New Testament.

52. The forceful demand for social justice by the prophets should by now be a commonplace (e.g. Isa. 5.7, etc.). We also are familiar with the centrality of the exodus, an experience of liberation and justice by an enslaved people, in the life and consciousness of the biblical people. But less known is that apart from 'love of God and love of neighbour', Jesus identified *justice-compassion-loyalty (read: 'social justice') as the weightier matters of the Torah*! Meditate on Matt. 23.23/ Luke 11.42 for this.

53. African and Asian spirituality must be drenched in *hope*. The biblical promise, especially the prophetic and apocalyptic vision, are our biblical sources for this hope.

Silence and contemplation

54. All this shows the cosmic nature, 'cosmicity' of biblical spirituality. However, all spirituality is incomplete without the dimension of *silence and contemplation*.

55. This bears emphasizing, in the light of the fact that contemplative silence is not part of the 'toolbox' of the average Christian, whereas it is a household item in the life and religion of the great faiths of the East. And yet, based on our experience of involvement in the work of justice and liberation, where the focus was on the outer world of history, we have come to appreciate the indispensability of interiority, the inner self, inner strength and growth and the inner journey. This silence, of course, should not lead to passivity and inactivity, but rather should energize us to become more integrated agents of change.

56. Jesus prayed. And our guess is that *Jesus prayed much in contemplative silence* – first, because he said 'When you pray, do not multiply words', second, because it is reported that he prayed all night, and how would an all-night prayer be if not mostly silent; third, because Jesus was a man of the East.

African and Asian spirituality and Jesus Christ

57. In our efforts to describe the African and Asian spirituality of our peoples, we need to relate Jesus Christ to the realities of our world. We note that the ultimate and radical uniqueness of Jesus is in his total self-donation in service to the other. His is a message and a saving example of love, which

he bequeathed to his community, the Church. Jesus preached and proclaimed the coming of the kingdom of God. 'Thy Kingdom Come', in which the resources of the world would be shared equitably: 'give us today our daily bread' and 'no one would be in need'.

58. Jesus of Nazareth was a human person who was loving and lovable, and committed to right relationships among all persons and with nature. The core of his teaching is that God is love, and those who love live in God. 'Love God and love your neighbour as yourself' is the supreme commandment, the fulfilment of the law and the prophets. In his ministry, Jesus proclaimed the divine presence in 'the least of these'. He made loving service to the other, especially the downtrodden of the world, the touchstone of spirituality and of union with God. Living a simple life-style close to nature, in a social context of inequality and harsh exploitation of women, the poor and the socially marginalized, he struggled unremittingly on their behalf. He gave his life as a witness to his uncompromising commitment to justice, equality, freedom, peace and authenticity. He began a community to bear witness to this message of love and example of authentic loving service.

59. With the passage of time, his identity and ministry were interpreted differently by the community of disciples. The role of the interpreting community is crucial for the presentation of Jesus and the mission of the Church. Different contextual theologies arise out of a community's ability to name and interpret Jesus' ministry within different contexts.

60. The Apostles recognized the Spirit in the centurion whom Peter visited and accepted to the community of believers by baptism, because the Spirit was already in him (Acts 10 and 11).

61. In the early church, there was a theology of Jesus, the Christ, that left room for the manifestation and presence of the Spirit of God in all persons, even before the coming of Jesus. Clement of Alexandria (150 – 211/216) writes: 'the authentic guides of humankind are the ancient philosophers who, truly inspired by God, acted upon by the Logos, have taught the nations divine truth . . . ', among them he mentions the Buddha (*Strom.* V,12, cf. Jacques Dupuis, *Jesus Christ and His Spirit*, Bangalore 1977, 15), cf. also the subordinationist and Nestorian traditions.

62. With the passage of centuries, the identity of Jesus was defined by the Councils as that of a divine-human being who is the Second Person of the Blessed Trinity of Father, Son and Holy Spirit. In the interpretation, Jesus was so divinized as to be the unique, exclusive, universal and final manifestation of God among humankind.

63. The dogmatic definitions of the Councils, along with the interpreta-

tion of original sin, did not apparently leave any room for God to operate salvifically among humans except through the ministrations of the church. They did not respect adequately the ineffable, inscrutable mystery of God who is above our human understanding and is the innermost being of all reality while also transcending them all.

64. Thus the Jesus presented to the African and Asian peoples by the Christian mission, following the Vasco da Gama enterprise, was *a Constantinian Jesus Christ*, with a harsh uncompromising judgment on African and Asian people who were not members of the Church and on their religions and cultures. This was due to the way Christian theology and spirituality had been evolved and practised over the centuries by a European Church favouring the Western white races as against the peoples of Africa and Asia.

65. Jesus Christ, understood in the Johannine and Pauline sense as the pre-existing Logos (John 1) and the one in whom all things are made and reconciled: 'For through him God created everything in heaven and on earth, the seen and the unseen things, including the spiritual powers, lords, rulers and authorities. God created the whole universe in him and for him. Christ existed before all things, and in union with him all things have their proper place' (Col. 1.16–17). Christ, the 'alpha and omega' of all things, is before the historical Jesus and is co-eternal with the 'Father' the Absolute Divinity. This Christ is not in contradiction to, or in competition with, the Absolute understood as transcendent in other religions and given different names as Yahweh. This is one manner in which the term *cosmic Christ* can be understood.

66. Another and different understanding of the Cosmic Christ, and also found in this document, is Jesus as interested in the human and the natural, the planet earth and the universe, the cosmos.

67. Traditional post-Constantinian theology soft-pedalled the social commitment of the historical Jesus and emphasized his transcendental divinity and insisted on his other-worldly salvific function in a context of a presupposition of a universally damning original sin. Once Jesus was thus removed from a struggling community, his message of liberation and his authority as God's human word (Logos) were diluted or neglected. He was used to legitimate exploitation of the worst type.

68. The awareness of the human identity, love-teaching and liberative mission of Jesus brings tremendous meaning to the peoples of Asia and Africa: this Jesus is indeed an earthly reality, always present in the many who are 'the least of these', the dispossessed.

69. Whereas Jesus Christ is not divided or divisive, the Jesus of Constantine, Columbus and Vasco da Gama has exported to Africa and

Asia the divisions and denominations of European socio-economic, patriarchal and theological power quarrels. We have different denominations because Europeans fought, and not because of the love message or example of Jesus.

70. We are aware of the scandal and limitations brought about by the growing divisions along ethnic and denominational lines which constitute a major weakness in understanding the historical ministry of Jesus. We need a *post-denominational and multi-cultural appropriation of the meaning of Jesus Christ*. This would bring about a new era for the Church's witness in the world where the key questions would be what Jesus would do if he were to re-appear among us once again, and what the rule of righteousness proclaimed by him means for us today.

71. The African and Asian peoples need to reacquire or retain their own indigenous cosmic spirituality, and the values of their great world religions along with Jesus of the Gospels, and what is positive in the ideologies. In so far as all religions and cultures have elements that are both enslaving and liberative we need to elaborate and apply principles for critically and constructively evaluating each and all of them. What is genuinely life-giving and fulfilling for humans and nature is from God the author of all good; and whatever human action is dehumanizing and devastating nature, the source of our life, is contrary to God's loving design for humankind and the cosmos.

Ecology, feminism and African and Asian spirituality

Towards a spirituality of Eco-Feminism

'Silence,
my soul,
these trees are prayers'

(*Rabindranath Tagore*)

72. One of the most important agendas for our time is how we can live with our mother earth promoting sustainability, diversity and balance. The earth is in danger. It is being destroyed with alarming speed. If this process is not stopped the next generation of living beings will have no livable earth to inherit. People who want to protect the earth and to promote the sustainable life style started the *ecological movement*, which challenges us to examine our way of thinking on nature, development and scientific progress. Ecologists enable us to see our anthropocentric sinfulness in relation to other living beings. They call us to the new relational pattern

based on mutuality, interdependence and life-giving values with all beings in the cosmos.

73. *Feminist movements* all over the world also have raised the most radical cultural critique of our way of living. They started naming the cause of women's pain and struggle with the conceptual framework called 'patriarchy'. Patriarchy is a hierarchical system of domination where men with power rule all other beings in the cosmos with their ideological invention of sexism, racism, classism, cultural imperialism and androcentrism. This system of 'domination-submission' has promoted war, injustice and ecological disaster in world history.

74. When the ecological movement and the feminist movement merged in a coalition to work toward justice, peace and the integrity of creation, they discovered that both movements shared many basic premises – such as their world view, analysis, method, life-style and vision of the future. Both movements are against any 'power-over' relationship which promotes dualistic, hierarchical oppressions among all beings. They envision a liberated and liberating relationship where 'power from within' and 'power with' other beings are encouraged. They think the rape of women and the rape of earth come from the same root. Both are based on the violence of 'power-over' which is the main characteristic of the man in power: he destroys the right relationship among all beings.

75. People who share both feminist and ecological world-view and participate in the movement for a feminist and ecological new world call themselves *'Eco-Feminists'* and their world-view *'Eco-Feminism'*; they draw their resources for struggle from more egalitarian, body-affirming, nature-respecting religions, cultures and ideologies. They are searching for a spirituality which promotes the immanence of God, the sacredness of this world and the wholeness of body, sensuality and sexuality. They want to rediscover the holiness of 'Matter' which has been prominent in many tribal and indigenous religions of the world. In their yearning for wholistic spirituality, eco-feminism and cosmic spirituality can empower each other.

Spirituality of primal religions

76. Many Eco-Feminists reject the spirituality of traditional Western Christianity which was based on Greek, Hellenistic dualism, hierarchy of beings and androcentric bias. Creation theology out of this tradition put human beings, specially man, at the centre of the universe. Man has 'dominion-over' all other beings in the cosmos. In this tradition God has been becoming increasingly the transcendental Other who has power – over the whole universe. This God has been used by many colonizers as an

ideological weapon for domination, exploitation and oppression. When God becomes a white, rich European man, white rich European man becomes a God for all other people and beings in the universe. Therefore Eco-Feminists are looking for an alternative spirituality which is able to respond to their need for affirming the sacredness of the cosmos.

77. Where can we find the resource for this cosmic spirituality? Many of us who participated in this conference agreed that institutionalized, patriarchal, other-worldly religions cannot be the main source of wholistic spirituality. *We turned to the spirituality of our indigenous people in Asia and Africa*. Their spirituality gives full values to creation as a dynamic and highly integrated Web of Life. It exudes life-giving values: sacredness of the land, reverence for all creatures, judicious use and conservation of the earth's resources, compassion for the weak, oppressed and marginalized. These cosmic values, rituals and practices are often considered 'superstitious'. But they capture a cosmic interwovenness that can become a healing and transforming experience for all of us.

A web of relationships

78. The cosmic interwovenness is a wholesome harmonious and compassionate web of relationships: intra-personal and inter-personal, communal and societal, global and planetary. This relationship is based on justice: No exploitation, or manipulation or oppression; *but mutuality, deep respect and delicate balance*. For example, when African and Asian people approach or pass rivers, trees, mountains, or when they plant, fish or harvest they often ask permission from the spirits of the land, the mountain, the plants and trees, the rivers and streams. They do not take from nature more than they need or without asking for what they need for life. They try to return to nature in some other way what they have taken, as if to repay this debt.

79. Therefore when *we incorporate African, Asian indigenous spirituality into Eco-Feminist spirituality*, we begin to perceive the meaning of nature, God and human in a fresh new way. First of all, Nature stops being a non-feeling, dead place. It becomes a God-infused and God-breathed place. We begin to feel deep respect, even a sense of awe before the life-giving, yet fragile interwovenness of the earth. The earth becomes sacred. The rhythmic ebb and flow of the rivers and seas becomes God's dance. The life-giving fecundity of the land with the water is the source of food coming from God's bosom. The wind and air become God's life-giving breath. Then we cannot destroy earth since God is there. God is the life-giving power. *The cosmos is God's 'womb'*. This intimate relationship

between God and the cosmos is exploding with seminal energy that generates and regenerates life. God energizes the cosmos, and the cosmos in return moves with the creator in a cosmic dance of exquisite balance and beauty. In this cosmic unfolding of ongoing creation, human beings become co-creators with God and nature.

80. This envisioning of *right relationship among God, human beings and nature* cannot just stay as an empowering image in the world of poetry. It should be incarnated in our people's struggle for survival and liberation empowering their life and movement. The feminist movement has always emphasized the meaning of 'personal is political'. When we ground our spirituality of Eco-Feminism in our everyday personal and political life orientating its energy to the liberation of the poor in the Third World, we will develop a concrete green life-style, green politics and economics. The cries of Nature from mountains deforested, rivers poisoned and air polluted due to Western-style development, multinational corporations and capitalism break our heart. The cries of women and children who become victims of sexual violence, tourism and poverty make us cry. Reaffirming our commitment to the struggle for liberation of our people and nature, we would like to close our statement by sharing the symbol of a tree. It is the most inspiring symbol for the spirituality of Eco-Feminism.

Symbol

81. The tree captures the life-giving thrust and power of the Eco-Feminist movement. Its roots go deep into the soil of Mother Earth, strengthening it against erosion yet sucking its life-giving moisture. Its trunk thrusts upwards into the freedom of the sky with consummate uniqueness in its texture, shape, size, its leaves, and its branches. The leaves transform death-dealing, poisonous carbon dioxide into life-giving oxygen. It provides shelter and shade for the life and growth of diverse insects, plants, birds, animals and humans. Its fruit gives food for body and its flower gives food for the soul. Then its leaves die and become manure to recreate the soil. This cyclic, rhythmic process of creating, nurturing, healing and recreating life symbolizes the aspirations of the cosmic spirituality of Eco-Feminism.

> 'I asked the tree,
> Speak to me about God,
> And it blossomed'
>
> (*Rabindranath Tagore*).

I Changed to Stay the Same
(Why I Left the Priesthood)

On 26 June 1992 I decided to change the path on which my life was moving, the path, not the direction, which continues unchanged. I detached myself from the presbyteral ministry and legally separated from the Order of Friars Minor.

This decision received widespread understanding from public opinion, and was supported by thousands of letters and petitions from every part of the world. In some circles there was also perplexity. I explained the reasons for this step in an open letter 'to my companions in faith and hope', and I do not wish to go over them again here. What I do want to do is describe the background to the issue, since it is something which transcends personal problems. Responsibility for personal decisions, with their absolute and in some ways mysterious character, can never be transferred, and I accept responsibility for this decision of mine before God and the world.

Many theologians of my generation are living through a deep crisis. We carried out our intellectual task under the influence of the innovating breeze brought by John XXIII and the Second Vatican Council. How we miss that jovial Pope and the first years of the pontificate of Paul VI! Under that torrent of freedom work which will surely stand as a landmark in the history of Christianity.

In Latin America, where the great majority of the world's Catholics live, movements and institutions grew up which carried the promise of a new model of church, free from the tyranny of the powers which had always colonized our peoples and yoked them to the dominant Western culture. Among these were the popular reading of the Bible, in which the poor regain possession of the Word to further their life and liberation; the church base communities, in which a new way of being church was worked out in practice, based more on communion, incarnate in the popular culture of Indians, mestizos and the poor; the social ministries, in which the liberating force of Christianity was rediscovered in the struggle against social injustice, the theology of liberation as the reflection necessary to accompany the action of Christians; and, coordinating this whole torrent of generosity, the bishops' conferences, in which the bishops, instead of authority figures, became pastors among their people, simple, prophetic and, a number of them, martyrs.

Then, from the end of the 1970s onwards, came the return to the grand ecclesiastical discipline. Groups in the Vatican bureaucracy which had been defeated but were still present in the power-structure succeeded in reorganizing. They produced their reading of the texts of Vatican II and with it a theological (ideological) justification for their Rome-centred centralizing activity. They projected a mythical aura round the figure of the Pope. They made him travel round the world, giving the faithful the impression that he was really the only bishop for the whole church and each individual. In the course of the 1980s, a skilful series of episcopal appointments changed the balance of bishop's conferences and isolated outstanding leaders. Theological work was made to conform, and a number of thinkers were disciplined. The whole church body was made uniform. A vast process of neo-Romanization and clericalization of the church was set in motion, only comparable with that which followed Vatican I.

Two models of the church are in conflict. The first, which derives from John XXIII and Vatican II, postulates the renewal of the church. It believes that the church needs to free itself from the historical weight of the centuries in order to be offered to every generation and enable them to have their encounter with the gospel, and for this it requires freedom and creativity. This gives rise to a polycentric view, that is, various centres of coordination and power. The second model starts from the conviction that the church does not need changes, but order and discipline to achieve an efficient spiritual conquest of modern culture. Discipline and order mean attitudes of obedience and submission to the strategies ordered by the authorities. This produces a monocentric model, that is, everything is to be thought and decided from a single centre in the Vatican.

The 1980s showed the imposition of the Roman model with the use of significant symbolic violence, as in the intervention to replace the elected leadership of CLAR (the Latin American Confederation of Religious), the dismantling of the prophetic, grass-roots based church of Archbishop Helder Câmara in Olinda and Recife, the overriding of venerable local traditions in Europe governing the appointment of bishops, strict control on the Africanization of the church in Africa, systematic suspicion and persecution of liberation theology.

This, it seems to me, is the structural background to the present tension in the Roman Catholic Church. Local and personal events take place within this framework. My decision can only be understood in terms of this situation. I have been on both sides of the divide. As a Franciscan priest I was part of the traditional hierarchical model of the church as organization; as a liberation theologian I became and continue to be part of the renewed model, church as community.

Because of my activity as a theologian and writer, director and adviser to the vast network of church base communities in Brazil and Latin America, from 1971 onwards I was placed under close surveillance by the Vatican's doctrinal authorities, always working in coordination with conservative groups in the local church, who supplied them with criticisms, complaints and accusations. Nothing comes from Rome without having first been sent there. In the beginning the letters came directly from the Cardinal Prefect of the Congregation for the Doctrine of the Faith to me. Then they only came through my general superior who, under pressure from above, put pressure on the local superior, who in turn put pressure on me. This cascade effect has a perversity all its own: it breaks the ties of fraternity between people, using them for functions which are not theirs, since a religious superior is not a doctrinal authority (i.e., not a bishop). In this way theological issues are settled by the vow of obedience: dialogue is replaced by submission, in the name of church discipline, 'for the good of the church, the Franciscan Order and the soul' (of the victim). I will repeat here what I wrote in my open letter. The personal experience I have acquired in these twenty years of dealings with doctrinal power is the following: it is cruel and without mercy. It forgets nothing, forgives nothing and exacts everything. Reading the records of my fellow-sufferers, from Galileo Galilei to Hans Küng or Eugen Drewermann, I find the same inquisitorial logic: arrogant, bureaucratic, cold and merciless.

Action is taken as though God did not exist and there was no humanity among human beings. In many letters there is no reference at all to God, Christ or anything divine. It is a refined form of sinning against the second commandment: taking God's holy name in vain by omitting his name but using its symbolic forces to steamroller the understanding of faith. I have the clear impression that we are witnessing a structural sin of the Roman Catholic institution, the claim to a monopoly of the truth and in its name the desire to control everything, even at the expense of human rights. Here there can be no conversion, because the conditions necessary for conversion have disappeared, namely humility, awareness of one's own fragility, readiness for mutual learning and respect for the divine mystery. Little or nothing of that exists here. The radical demands of the gospel have been replaced by mere rigorism.

This type of ecclesiastical behaviour brings the church closer to the palaces of Caesars than Peter's humble boat. The sense of impotence and despair come to dominate a theologian's life. This type of church has no salvation to offer.

How can they say, as conservative thinking does: outside the church no salvation? I am appalled at the thought that this type of church and behaviour might perpetuate itself until the end of the world. What have we done with Jesus' legacy of fraternity and tenderness, which reveal the maternal and paternal face of God?

On the other hand, as a theologian who is part of the church-as-community (within which there are people ranging from cardinals and cultivated people to the vast mass of believing Catholics) I felt that not all was lost. Here one can live a little of Jesus' dream of a fraternal and sororal community. The great majority of members of this people's church (so-called because it is part of the people of God) come from the great tribulation of life, are poor and excluded. Their concerns are not those of discipline, order and orthodoxy, but the relationship between the gospel and injustice, between the God of life and the poor. In fellowship and sharing life and faith with them, there is a constant new enthusiasm and a great sense of vitality. Life is too short for all the tasks we have to perform together.

When I saw that the possibilities for action and reflection within the church as great institution had almost all been closed to me, I decided to resign the functions I used to perform within it as a Franciscan religious and presbyter. In some situations the important thing is not to know whether or not we have succeeded in changing the church institution, but to have the courage not to let it change us. I prefer the risk which forces me to be creative to the accommodation which brings a tranquillity unrelated to the gospel spirit.

I changed so that I could continue to be the same, that is, to accompany the communities, do theology in close contact with action, celebrate faith and hope in the communities, which in Brazil are numbered in their thousands. I have not resigned from this; on the contrary, this is my spiritual home. On this level I continue to be a presbyter and a Franciscan.

In the end we only pass through this life once, and it needs to be worth living, especially in the freedom of Christ won for us at the price of his own blood. I feel myself a theologian of the Christian community, which is greater than the organized church. I continue to join in the activities of the communities, including their worship, because they welcome me as they always did.

At the Eighth Inter-Ecclesial Meeting of Base Communities, held in September 1992 in Santa Maria, in the south of Brazil, attended by three thousand representatives from Brazil and the whole of Latin America, my presence was insisted on. I returned early from Switzerland in response to this insistence, which was backed by the bishops present there. The welcome, the applause and the community prayer meant for me a sort of re-consecration to the service of the people of God and the people's church.

I realize that my decision implies a relativizing of stages of my past, not from infidelity to what I promised before, but in search for a path in accordance with my conscience. This path seeks sustenance from the same root from which spring baptismal consecration, the presbyteral ministry and the Franciscan charism: discipleship of Jesus, the enthusiasm of the Spirit and communion with all in the great communion of the Trinity.

Leonardo Boff
Translated by Francis McDonagh

The editors of the Special Column are Norbert Greinacher and Bas van Iersel. The content of the Special Column does not necessarily reflect the views of the Editorial Board of Concilium.

Contributors

TEOTONIO R. DE SOUZA joined the Society of Jesus in 1967. After studying Portuguese and philosophy he gained his MA and PhD from the University of Pune. Since 1979 he has been Founder-Director of the Xavier Centre of Historical Research in Goa and guides PhD research at Goa University. He is a fellow of the Portuguese Academy of History in Lisbon, the Heras Institute of Indian History and Culture in Bombay and the Menezes Braganza Institute in Goa, and visiting professor of the Vidyajyoti Institute of Religions in Delhi, as well as General Co-ordinator of the EATWOT Commission on Church History. In addition to writing many articles and editing several books he is author of *Medieval Goa* (1979).

Address: Xavier Centre of Historical Research, Alto Porvorim, Goa 503 521, India.

SAMUEL RAYAN was born in 1920, entered the Society of Jesus in 1939 and after a degree in literature at the University of Irivandrum was ordained priest in 1955. He gained his doctorate in theology at the Gregorian University in Rome and from 1961 to 1972 was chaplain to the University Students Organization in Kerala; since 1972 he has been Professor of Theology at Vidya Jyoti, Delhi. He served on the WCC Commission on Faith and Order from 1968 to 1982 and is sectional editor of the theological journal *Jeevadhara*. In addition to articles he has written *The Holy Spirit*, New York 1978; *The Anger of God*, Bombay 1982; and *In Christ: The Power of Women*, Madras 1986.

Address: Vidya Jyoti, 23 Raj Niwas Marg, Delhi 11054, India.

KWOK PUI-LAN received her doctorate from Harvard University and teaches theology at Episcopal Divinity School, Cambridge, Mass. She has lectured on Asian feminist theology in many parts of the world. She is the author of *Chinese Women and Christianity, 1860–1927*, and co-editor of *Inheriting our Mothers' Gardens: Feminist Theology in Third World*

Perspective. Her articles also appear in *Semeia*, *Concilium* and the *East Asian Journal of Theology*.

Address: 99 Brattle Street, Cambridge, MA 02138, USA.

ALOYSIUS PIERIS, a Sri Lankan Jesuit, was born in 1934. He is the founder-director of the Tulana Research Centre in Kelaniya near Colombo. A classical Indologist who has specialized in Buddhist philosophy, he is now engaged in a vast research programme on mediaeval Pali (Buddhist) philosophical literature, on which he has begun publishing a series of papers. He edits *Dialogue*, an international review for Buddhists and Christians published by the Ecumenical Institute, Colombo. He has written extensively on missiology, theology of religions, Asian theology of liberation and Buddhology. He is the author of *An Asian Theology of Liberation* (New York 1988) and *Love Meets Wisdom* (New York 1988). He is visiting professor at the Asian Pastoral Institute, Manila and has also held the Franciscan Chair of Mission Studies at Washington Theological Union (1987), the Henry Luce Chair of World Christianity at Union Theological Seminary, New York (1988) and the Ann Potter Wilson Distinguished Chair of Theology at Vanderbilt University, Nashville (1992).

Address: Tulana Research Centre, Kohalwila Road, Gonawala, Kelaniya, Sri Lanka.

FELIX WILFRED was born in India in 1948. He is Professor of Systematic Theology in St Paul's Seminary, Tiruchirapalli and visiting professor at the East Asian Pastoral Institute, Manila, and also a former president of the Indian Theological Association. His works include *Emergent Church in a New India, Sunset in the East?, Asian Challenges and Christian Involvement,* and *Theologiegeschichte der Dritten Welt: Indien*.

Address: St Paul's Seminary, P.O. Box 36, Tiruchirapalli 62001, India.

CARLOS H. ABESAMIS studied theology at Innsbruck University and scripture at the Pontifical Biblical Institute in Rome. Since 1968 he has taught scriptural courses at various theological schools and holds seminars and workshops on re-reading the Bible in the Third World. He is Co-founder of the Socio-Pastoral Institute and a founder member of the Ecumenical Association of Third World Theologians. In addition to a number of articles he has written *A Third Look at Jesus*, Quezon City, revised edition 1991.

Address: Loyola House of Studies, PO Box 4082, Manila, Philippines.

FRANCIS X. D'SA is an Indian Jesuit who has studied at the University of Pune, India, and the universities of Innsbruck and Vienna, Austria. He is Professor of Systematic Theology and Indian Religions at the Jnana Deepa Vidyapeeth (Pontificium Athenaeum), Pune, and is Director of the Institute for the Study of Religion there. He was guest lecturer at the University of India for more than a decade and has lectured at various European universities. Though he edits a series of concordances of Sanskrit religious texts, his main interest is in cross-cultural studies. In addition to a book on an Indian hermeneutical school he is the author of *Gott, der Dreieine und der All-Ganze*. Recent publications (e.g. on human rights, dharma) are all from a cross-cultural perspective.

Address: Institute for the Study of Religion, c/o De Nobili College, Post Box 7, Ramwadi, Pune 411 014, India.

MARY JOHN MANANZAN is the National Chairperson of Gabriela, a national federation of women's organizations in the Philippines. She is also Dean of College of St Scholastica's College and Director of the Institute of Women's Studies. She is co-foundress of the Citizen's Alliance for Consumer Protection, of which she is the present Secretary General, and the Center for Women's Resources, of which she is the present Chairperson of the Board of Advisers. She has just been elected International Coordinator of the Women's Commission of the Ecumenical Association of Third World Theologians (EATWOT).

Address: St Scholastica's College, 2560 Leon Guinto Street, PO Box 3153, D–406 Manila, Philippines.

MAI THANH was born of a Confucian family and converted to Christianity. She studied theology at the Institut Catholique in Paris and philosophy at the Sorbonne, gaining her doctorate on television and education in Paris, where she also became a member of the Notre Dame Congregation. In Vietnam she taught philosophy in schools and was appointed professor in the university of Dalat. Before 1975 she was responsible for adult educational programmes transmitted by the Jesuit-run Alexander of Rhodes Centre; from then until 1984 she ran children's education programmes at the state television centre in Ho Chi Minh City. She is now in the service of her Congregation and temporarily resident in France.

Address: 8 Avenue Daniel Lesueur, Paris 75007, France. 228 Nam ky khoi nghia, Ho Chi Minh City, Vietnam.

PETER NEMESHEGYI was born in Budapest in 1923; he studied law and constitutional law at the State University of Budapest and philosophy and theology in Szeged, Innsbruck and Rome. He gained his doctorate in theology at the Papal Gregorian University in Rome and since 1956 has been teaching fundamental and dogmatic theology at the Sophia University, Tokyo. He is the author of *La paternité de Dieu chez Origène* and has written many theological books and articles, especially in Japanese and Hungarian.

Address: 2–7–10 Sekimachi-Higashi, Nerima-ku, Tokyo 177, Japan.

TISSA BALASURIYA was born in Sri Lanka in 1924 and studied in the universities of Ceylon, Rome, Oxford and Paris. From 1964 to 1971 he was Rector of Aquinas University College, and from 1969 to 1979 Asian Chaplain of Catholic Students Pax Romana; since 1971 he has been Founder/Director of the Centre for Society and Religion; he was also a founder member of the Ecumenical Association of Third World Theologians, being its Asian co-ordinator from 1976 to 1986. He edits several journals and has written many pamphlets and articles; his books include *Jesus Christ and Human Liberation* (1976), *Eucharist and Human Liberation* (1977), *Planetary Theology* (1984), *Mary and Human Liberation* (1990) and *Right Relationships: De-Routing and Re-Rooting of Christian Theology* (1991).

Address: Centre for Society and Religion, 281 Deans Road, Colombo 10, Sri Lanka 1.

Members of the Advisory Committee for Theology of the Third World

Directors

Leonardo Boff OFM	Rio de Janeiro	Brazil
Virgil Elizondo	San Antonio, Texas	USA

Members

K. C. Abraham	Bangalore	India
Hugo Assmann	Piracicaba	Brazil
Frank Chikane	Braamfontein	South Africa
Zwinglio Mota Dias	Rio de Janeiro RJ	Brazil
Enrique Dussel	Mexico, DF	Mexico
Gustavo Gutiérrez	Lima	Peru
François Houtart	Louvain-la Neuve	Belgium
Joâo Batista Libanio SJ	Belo-Horizonte MG	Brazil
Beatriz Melano Couch	Buenos Aires	Argentina
José Miguez Bonino	Buenos Aires	Argentina
Uriel Molina	Managua	Nicaragua
Ronaldo Muñoz	Santiago	Chile
John Mutiso-Mbinda	Rome	Italy
Alphonse Mgindu Mushete	Kinshasa, Limeta	Zaire
M. A. Odyoye	Geneva	Switzerland
Soon-Kyung Park	Seoul	Korea
Juan Hernandez Pico SJ	Mexico, DF	Mexico
Aloysius Pieris SJ	Gonawala-Kalaniya	Sri Lanka
Samual Rayan SJ	Delhi	India
Pabo Richard	San José	Costa Rica
J. Russel Chandran	Bangalore	India
Anselme Titianma Sanon	Bobo-Dioulassa	Upper Volta
Jon Sobrino	San Salvador	El Salvador

Concilium

Issues of *Concilium* to be published in 1993

Messianism through History
Edited by Wim Beuken, Sean Freyne and Anton Weiler

Explores the role that the notion of a Messiah has played in determining Jewish and Christian self-identities through history. After a first section on the latest understanding of the biblical background it traces messianic thought in Judaism and Christianity in the Middle Ages before discussing the implications of messianic belief today.

03018 8   *1993/1*   *February*

Any Room for Christ in Asia?
Edited by Leonardo Boff and Virgil Elizondo in collaboration with Aloysius Pieris and Mary-John Mananzan

In Asia, Christians are a very small percentage of the people. Is this inevitable? A first section looks at the guises in which 'Christ' entered Asia and non-Christian perceptions of Christ; this is followed by accounts of specific current theological interpretations of Christ in Asian churches.

03019 6   *1993/2*   *April*

The Spectre of Mass Death
Edited by David N. Power

How does Christianity repond to catastrophes involving the sudden deaths of thousands: war, famine and flood or epidemics like AIDS and drugs? This issue begins with examples of how people do in fact react, considers traditional responses to the question of evil in this connection, and then considers possible liturgical remembrance and forms of prayer.

03020 X   *1993/3*   *June*

Reincarnation or Resurrection?
Edited by Hermann Häring and Johann-Baptist Metz

A first part considers varieties of ideas of reincarnation in Hinduism, Buddhism, Latin America and African religion, and the popularity of reincarnation in modern belief; a second part adopts a similar approach to ideas of resurrection; the final part compares and contrasts the two approaches.

03021 8   *1993/4*   *August*

Migrants and Refugees
Edited by Norbert Greinacher and Norbert Mette

The mass migration of people, especially in the Third World, as a result of war, famine or other pressures, is a major problem for the world. This issue offers accounts of what is actually happening on various continents, analyses the sociology of migration, considers the ethical issues and outlines possible Christian responses.

03022 6   1993/5   October

Mass Media
Edited by John A. Coleman and Miklos Tomka

This issue recognizes that the media represent a complex phenomenon requiring deeper analysis than the church is often prepared to give. It seeks to help readers to understand better how the media work, how media communication should be 'read' and the moral and value issues involved in debates on the media.

03023 4   1993/6   December

Titles for Issues to be Published in 1994

1994/1   **Violence against Women**

1994/2   **Christianity and Culture: A Mutual Enrichment**

1994/3   **Islam: A Challenge for Christianity**

1994/4   **Mysticism and the Institutional Crisis**

1994/5   **Catholic Identity**

1994/6   **Why Theology?**

Back Issues of *Concilium* still available

All listed issues are available at £6.95/US$15.00 each. Add 10% of value for postage.
Special rates are sometimes available for large orders. Please write for details.

1965

1   Dogma ed. Schillebeeckx: *The very first issue*
2   Liturgy On the Vatican Constitution: *Jungmann and Gelineau*
3   Pastoral ed. Rahner: *The first issue on this topic*
4   Ecumenism: *Küng on charismatic structure, Baum on other churches*
5   Moral Theology: *Its nature: law, decalogue, birth control*
6   Church and World: *Metz, von Balthasar, Rahner on ideology*
7   Church History: *Early church, Constance, Trent, religious freedom*
8   Canon Law: *Conferences and Collegiality*
9   Spirituality: *Murray Rogers, von Balthasar: East and West*
10   Scripture Inspiration and Authority; *R.E. Murphy, Bruce Vawter*

1966

11   Dogma Christology: *Congar, Schoonenberg, Vorgrimler*
12   Liturgy: *The liturgical assembly, new church music*
13   Pastoral Mission after Vatican 2
14   Ecumenism: *Getting to know the other churches*
15   Moral Theology Religious Freedom: *Roland Bainton, Yves Congar*
16   Church and World Christian Faith v. Atheism: *Moltmann, Ricoeur*
17   Church History: *Jansenism, Luther, Gregorian Reform*
18   Religious Freedom In Judaism, Hinduism, Spain, Africa
19   Religionless Christianity? *Bernard Cooke, Duquoc, Geffre*
20   Bible and Tradition: *Blenkinsopp, Fitzmeyer, P. Grelot*

1967

21   Revelation and Dogma: *A reconsideration*
23   Atheism and Indifference: *Includes two Rahner articles*
24   Debate on the Sacraments: *Thurian, Kasper, Ratzinger, Meyendorff*
25   Morality, Progress and History: *Can the moral law develop?*
26   Evolution: *Harvey Cox, Ellul, Rahner, Eric Mascall*
27   Church History: *Sherwin-White and Oberman; enlightenment*
28   Canon Law - Theology and Renewal: *Hopes for the new Canon Law*
29   Spirituality and Politics: *Balthasar; J.A.T. Robinson discussed*
30   The Value of the OT: *John McKenzie, Munoz Iglesias, Coppens*

1968

31   Man, World and Sacrament: *Congar, J.J.Hughes on Anglican orders*
32   Death and Burial: *Theology and Liturgy*
33   Preaching the Word of God: *Congar, Rahner on demythologizing*
34   Apostolic by Succession? *Issues in ministry*
35   The Church and Social Morality: *Major article by Garaudy*
36   Faith and Politics: *Metz, Schillebeeckx, Leslie Dewart*
37   Prophecy: *Francis of Assisi, Ignatius of Loyola, Wesley, Newman*
38   Order and the Sacraments: *Confirmation, marriage, bishops*

Please send remittances and any enquiries to:
SCM Press Ltd, 26-30 Tottenham Road, London N1 4BZ

Concilium Subscription Information

Individual Annual Subscription (six issues): £30.00

Institution Annual Subscription (six issues): £40.00

Airmail subscriptions: add £10.00

Individual issues: £8.95 each

New subscribers please return this form:
for a two-year subscription, double the appropriate rate

(for individuals)   £30.00   (1/2 years)   . . . .

(for institutions)   £40.00   (1/2 years)   . . . .

Airmail postage
outside Europe +£10.00   (1/2 years)   . . . .

Total . . . .

I wish to subscribe for one/two years as an individual/institution
(delete as appropriate)

Name/Institution . . . .

Address . . . .

. . . .

. . . .

I enclose a cheque for . . . . payable to SCM Press Ltd

Please charge my Access/Visa/Mastercard no. . . . .

Signature . . . . .Expiry Date . . . .

Please return this form to:
SCM PRESS LTD 26-30 Tottenham Road, London N1 4BZ